Law of Attraction Secrets:

Success and Nothing Less Science

The Power of Creating Your Own Reality

Law of Attraction
SECRETS

Success and Nothing Less Science
The Power of Creating Your Own Reality

by Robert and Rachael Zink

LAW OF ATTRACTION SECRETS:

SUCCESS AND NOTHING LESS SCIENCE.

THE POWER OF CREATING YOUR OWN REALITY

by Robert and Rachael Zink

Law of Attraction Solutions, LLC
2016

First Edition: 2016
ISBN 978-0-9908250-4-3

Published by

Law of Attraction Solutions, LLC

3439 NE Sandy Blvd #124

Portland, OR 97232

www.lawofattractionsolutions.com

Dedicated to my wonderful wife Rachael,

who inspires me to reach for the stars.

May this book inspire you

the way she inspires me.

TABLE OF CONTENTS

ACKNOWLEDGMENTS

I, Robert Zink, have an untold number of people and experiences to thank for the creation of this book. I would like to keep this simple and just mention people who got their hands dirty with me in the creation of this book, <u>Law of Attraction Secrets: Success and Nothing Less Science</u>. There is not enough space in this acknowledgment to mention all of you but know that I appreciate all you have done for me.

The content of this book is my core thoughts and beliefs as I recorded on audio through the years on my Talk Radio Podcast called "Law of Attraction Secrets". Katrina Rundle started the process of turning my audio into print. She transcribed twenty podcast that soon became the base for each chapter in this book. Katrina is a true testament to the power of the Law of Attraction. It was through Miracle Mentoring & Alchemy Life Coaching that Katrina tapped into her true potential. She left everything she knew to go to Thailand to teach English and learn yoga. Katrina is now back in the States living her dream as a yoga instructor and school teacher.

It did not take me long to realize that the audio Katrina transcribed needed many hours of rewriting to create a smooth flowing book. My lovely wife Rachael, whom I dedicated this book to, did most of the rewriting. It was her labor intensive efforts that took this book from audio to print. She added endless number of explanation sentences which filled in the gaps that could only be understood by the vocal inflection found in the audio. When I compared the audio transcripts with Rachael's expanded version, I knew that she must be listed as a co-author. My deepest thanks goes out to her for her dedication in making my dream of a Law of Attraction book a reality.

I must also thank those that edited my manuscript, Victoria Generao and Kendall Blythe. Their ability to find the grammar and punctuation issues put a little extra juice in the book. I am grateful for their ongoing encouragement, pushing me to continue to write.

As for those that planted the seeds of attraction and energy manipulation in my life I send my love to the late Donald Michael Kraig, Israel Regardie, Don Squire, Wayne Dyer, and my two amazing Grandmothers. Every Miracle Mentoring client I have ever spoken to has also played a role in the creation of this book. These are the people I have helped in all 50 States and 60 different countries of the world empower their life.

I also want to thank you the reader for your interest in this book. I would love to receive your feedback, questions, and comments via email to lawofattractionsolutions@gmail.com. It is for you that I write and share the wisdom of success sciences & the magic of Inner Light. Without you the reader, none of this would be possible.

To all those that remain unmentioned, thank you. May you be inspired and attract your wildest dreams.

FORWARD

Written by

Million Dollar Lottery Winner

& Business Entrepreneur

Amanda Spiller

If you are struggling and seeking a new direction you have found the right place to start. This book is just a taste of all the Law of Attraction knowledge and secrets Robert Zink has to share with the world. Believe me I know first-hand. I am Amanda Spiller and would like to share with you how Robert has been a great influence in my life. He has helped me in huge ways to attract the life I desire.

Earlier this year, I decided that I was in need of some motivation and education. I wanted quality information on the Law of Attraction from a podcast so that I could listen to it while getting ready for work. Thank goodness Robert's Law of Attraction podcast called "Law of Attraction Secrets" was one of the first search results in iTunes. It is concise and jam-packed with useful, practical, and inspirational content. After a short time of listening, I decided to try some of Robert's audio programs available for instant download at www.lawofattractionsolutions.com. I purchased the programs called "Chakra Cleaning" and "Money Like Magic". I also purchased the personal alchemy program called, "The Guarantee." After using these programs and noticing changes in my life and the way I felt, I made the decision to work with Robert as my Miracle Mentor and Alchemy Life Coach. I hired Robert two months after beginning listening to those podcasts, and it was one of the best decisions of my life.

When I began working with Robert I was not making the income I wanted to make and I was unhappy with the amount of time I had to work to make it. My relationship had just ended. I was lacking focus on what I wanted to do in my business and had no strong boundaries in my personal life and relationships. With Robert's help, I have set clear boundaries for myself and I do not go back on them. I have greater clarity on what to do in my businesses and where to go with them. Robert has helped me begin and grow a great network marketing venture for a product I am very passionate about. I am following my true desire to start a wellness coaching and aromatherapy based business. I am also very happily back with my partner in a relationship that is better now than I could have ever imagined it before.

After just 8 weeks of being mentored by Robert, I received my first big miracle. Some things had happened before this one that I considered miraculous and was incredibly grateful for, but this one was a doozy. I attracted a very large, unexpected amount of money into my life. This money has allowed me to pay off debt, invest in my businesses, invest in a better life for my family, save, be comfortable, and have fun! There is no doubt in my mind that the changes in my beliefs and thought processes allowed this miracle to occur. The work that I put in and the knowledge that I gained from Robert changed my life FOREVER.

The Law of Attraction is always working. Make it work for you. This book will give you the tools you need to start attracting the life you desire. Every chapter is filled with practical, hands on techniques to change your thinking and attraction power.

What I love about this book is that every chapter can be read as its own meditation. You could read one chapter a week and take seven days to implement the teachings before reading the next chapter. I am certain that if you do this, your life will change for the better before you are half way done reading this book. Law of Attraction Secrets: Success and Nothing Less Science is not a fluffy, feel good book. It is a book of golden nuggets of truth and hard facts that force you to take action on your goals.

Thank you, Robert, for getting me to "put skin in the game".

Amanda Spiller

Miracle Mentoring & Alchemical Life Coaching Client

PREFACE

Law of Attraction Secrets: Success and Nothing Less Science is a long time coming. I, Robert Zink, have been sharing Law of Attraction Secrets and teaching energy manipulation for decades now. My training in energy manipulation started in learning the ancient mysteries through the teachings of the Order of the Golden Dawn. For many years, I have been Imperator General of the Esoteric Order of the Golden Dawn. As my knowledge of energy grew, I became enlightened with how energy manipulation could be used in healing the body and eradicating disease. This led to the founding of the Ruach Healing Method, which is the subject of my first book **Magical Energy Healing: The Ruach Healing Method.**

In these roles, I learned how to communicate the foundation and secrets of the Law of Attraction as found in the Emerald Tablet of Hermes. I have been communicating this knowledge in my podcast "The Secret Temple" found on Blog Talk Radio and iTunes since 2009. These podcasts are now entitled "Law of Attraction Secrets". Radio is my first passion for sharing information but in my growth, I recognize the timelessness of writing. Until recent technologies, it was the simple form of writing by candle light or word of mouth that brought the ancient teaching and wisdom of the Law of Attraction down through the ages.

My purpose in writing this book is to continue to share my knowledge and passion for the Law of Attraction. I believe that you need more than just your average life coach or Law of Attraction guru. True, life-altering change comes from an understanding of the deep, ancient mysteries of attraction. In writing this book, I seek to share this knowledge with a greater portion of the world than I do on my podcast. I want everyone to have the information necessary to achieve their heart's true desires. When you actualize your true potential and desires, you are empowered to change the world.

This book springs from those podcasts. In this way, <u>Law of Attraction Secrets: Success and Nothing Less Science</u> does not have to be read cover to cover. Each chapter is designed as its own mini-lesson in the Law of Attraction. Please use the table of contents to find chapters that meet your current situation. Read the chapter thoroughly, perhaps with a highlighter, so that the great truths sink deep into your subconscious mind, then put the knowledge into action. You may choose not read another chapter until you have completely applied all the lesson from the chapter you choose.

As you read through each chapter, you will notice themes that affect all Law of Attraction work repeated. It will not take you long to understand the importance of the phrase "As above, so below." I repeat this information for two reasons. The first is because of the extreme significance of the information as it affects how you attract the life you desire. The second is so that each chapter can be read as its own lesson.

Throughout this book you will find examples of people that have taken action to empower their dreams and those that have not taken action. All of the examples in this book are true stories from my personal life and years of mentoring. Some of the names have been changed to protect the identity of my clients. I hope that these examples inspire you beyond your wildest dreams.

I am always here for you. Help is on the way. All you have to do is seek it out. Please enjoy, learn, and share the truths in this book. I would love to get your feedback. Please write me at lawofattractionsolutions@gmail.com.

Sincerely,

Robert A. Zink

Founder of Miracle Mentoring & Alchemical Life Coaching

Imperator General of the Esoteric Order of the Golden Dawn

Creator of the Ruach Healing Method

CHAPTER 1: IMAGINATION, CREATIVITY & BODY-MIND SECRETS OF THE LAW OF ATTRACTION

"That's the real trouble with the world,

too many people grow up."

Walt Disney

The Law of Attraction can radically change the course of your life in a positive way. This chapter will touch upon some important points. Apply these points now, to witness the kind of results you desire in your life. See them come to fruition within months, weeks, or perhaps even hours.

Let me share a story. Not long ago, I mentored a gentleman who was seeking more income. A couple of hours after our phone session, he called back to announce that he had made one of his biggest sales ever. This big sale saved his business and because of his success, he was not just surviving, he was thriving.

I have been know as the "Mentor of Light" for many years through my involvement in the mystery traditions of the Golden Dawn. Several of my friends and clients gave me this name which has become a standard I have worked to live up to.

When we think of the Law of Attraction, often we don't think of the mysteries which hark back to Ancient Egypt and beyond, yet we should. The Law of Attraction is not new. You might be surprised to find that the core principles of the Law of Attraction are actually found in the ancient teachings of Hermes. In the Emerald Tablet it states, "As above, so below". Another interpretation of that is "As within, so without". In other words, what is inside of you is also what is outside of you. What you have created in your inner, microcosmic world is what you will see in the outer, macrocosmic world. The truth is that if you are not happy and exhilarated with the life you have right now – your finances, relationships, friendships – then the wrong energy is filing your inner world and is manifesting in your outside world.

Think of the Law of Attraction as a huge magical magnet and every thought that you think – good, bad or indifferent – has a counterpart that ends up in your life. I'm often reminded of individuals who transform a large white board into what they call a "wish board". Wish board creators search through hundreds of magazines looking for pictures that express their desires. In addition, they will write down what they want specifically. The process of building a wish board gives the creators positive juice flowing through their energy field. When the wish board is hung up in their office or bedroom, they often feel exhilarated.

Then, the same wish board creator goes outside to check the mailbox and discovers a stack of bills! Suddenly, all those demonizing thoughts of poverty consciousness come back into their mentality. Poverty re-permeates the wish board creator's mind and sets up a counter-intention. A counter-intention is an intention pointing you in the opposite direction of where you desire to go. YOU DON'T HAVE TO LIVE THAT WAY. The fact of the matter is, you CAN have the life you desire, you CAN make a difference in this world, and you CAN have the type of happiness you crave. The Law of Attraction empowers you to wake up every day exhilarated about living the life you deeply desire.

Let's examine several absolutely critical factors in activating the Law of Attraction. The first is *imagination*. Most of us don't give imagination the kind of importance that it deserves in manifesting an extraordinary life. How many times have you heard someone say, "It's just a figment of your imagination!"? You've heard those kinds of words before? Maybe you are guilty of using them yourself, maybe even with your children.

Think of young children; they have an almost unlimited imagination with no boundaries. Children don't think in terms of boundaries or limitations. It is only through time, experience, teaching, parents, school, and society that they create limitations. These boundaries literally choke the imagination. When you choke the imagination, you choke your ability to attract what you really desire in your life.

Albert Einstein said, "Imagination is the preview of life's coming attractions." Albert Einstein was a very creative and imaginative individual. He struggled with the whole Law of Relativity and the concept of light but couldn't quite get a grasp on it. He said it was *only* when he got *out* of his analytical mind and began to visualize himself riding on a beam of light that he could understand the concept of light and mass. Of course, the famous Theory of Relativity developed from there. Did this theory develop from the left-brain? No, it developed from the right-brain, the imaginative part of the brain that we try to squash and bury in our modern analytical world.

Think about this for a moment: Walt Disney believed that imagination was the key to life. He actually had a formula for allowing the imagination to go unchecked. How do we maximize the imagination's creativity? We want to give it some direction, but we don't want to hold it back. How does a creative imagination work?

First, sit down with a pen and paper and think about what is important to you. Then, write down the things that you do not desire in your life. Let's say, you come up with six primary things that you do NOT desire. Understand that you are not going to stay in that negative mindset. However, knowing what you don't desire is a key to better understanding what you DO desire.

The ancient mystics, before they began invoking anything of a positive nature, would always do a formal banishing of the negative. This can be done through cleansing rites, smudging, the Lesser Banishing Ritual of the Pentagram or other rites. All of these kinds of cleansing rites are designed to banish the unwanted.

You can't put new wine in an old wine skin. You need to clear the cup of your subconscious mind first, then you will be prepared to hold the elixir of your life. First, sit down and write down the experiences you don't desire in a particular area of your life. Next, engage in some *"mental judo"*. After you write down something you don't want, convert it into something you DO want. In this way, you crop off the things you don't want by eliminating the negative. For example, if you were starting a business, you might say, "I don't want to work 20 hours a day opening up a new business." You have now determined what you don't want. Now, write that thought in the form of a statement of what you do want, "I am working a comfortable number of hours a day and making an extraordinary profit." This new statement becomes your positive affirmation. Notice that this affirmation is in the present tense, beginning with the two words "I am". In writing your affirmation, you might get even more specific with the amount of profit you desire.

You never say what you don't want as an affirmation, but you have to understand what you don't want so you can convert it into what you do want. Another example: "I don't want to be fat." It's not healthy to stay in that mind frame. Invert the phrase to "I am becoming skinny", or "I am becoming healthy", or "I have a proportionate body or attractive body".

You are now giving yourself a path for your imagination to go wild. Go ahead let your imagination go wild! Allow your imagination to simply go unchecked. It is very important to understand that when you allow your imagination to go unchecked, when you start to visualize and emotionalize what you want, you must first warn your left-brain. Talk to your left-brain about turning off for just a moment. Say, "Look, you're going to get a chance to come look at this issue later on, but right now, just stay out of it long enough so that the imaginative side of me can go unchecked." Make friends with your left-brain. Tell the left-brain that it will get its chance later on, but right now, it's the right brain's turn. You don't want to put the brakes on the imagination; you want it to flow as fast and as freely as it is able.

I've worked with advertising and marketing businesses for many years. Often, my colleagues and I would have giant pieces of white paper covered with thousands of scribbles as we synergized ideas and allowed our imaginations to go unchecked. That's how you come up with great advertising and clever ideas. With regards to the Law of Attraction and getting what you desire in life, you have to be at a point where you emotionalize, see, feel, hear, smell and experience the life you crave. As the imagination is given unrestricted time to create, you begin to invoke *sub-modalities*. Sub-modalities are ways to process information like sights, sound, feel, smell, and taste. All of these senses are very important. The more sub-modalities or senses you can evoke in your creative visualization, the better you can imprint that into yourself to begin attracting what you desire through the abundance of the Universe.

The second critical factor in activating the Law of Attraction is to *own your creativity*. Allow your thoughts to create. I talk to people all the time through Miracle Mentoring and Alchemy Life Coaching who say, "Robert, I want to find myself!" "Good, I'm glad you want to find yourself." However, there is an action that is more important than *finding* yourself. This action is clearing some of the past pain and limiting beliefs, then starting with a clean slate you can begin *creating* yourself. You are co-creator with the Universe. You can create yourself into just about anything you desire. You have the ability to create yourself, create the life you desire and to create yourself from the inside out. It's not about creating things that you're attracting into your life; it's about creating what you desire on a soul level.

You're not on a journey of self-discovery; you're on a

journey of self-creation. This is the key to a masterful life. Your journey is about creating who you are and the life you desire. Therefore, as you begin to understand that, in using your imagination, you are CREATING who and what you desire to be, not merely discovering who you are, you realize that you unlock unlimited power and potential. This realization alone opens you up to attracting more of what you desire in your life.

Deepak Chopra says, "We are not onlookers peering into a unified field of separate objective reality. We are the unified field; every thought you are thinking creates a weight in the unified field." My question to you is this: How important is it for you to monitor your creativity? It's essentially important! Many people say, "I'm working all the time with these positive thoughts but I'm still not getting what I want." There are some other reasons for that and they are always able to be addressed through hypnosis or some other form of deep mind therapy. Think of your mind as an iceberg. The tip of the iceberg is consciousness and you have to take control of that. You also have an unlimited subconscious which takes the majority of the responsible for creating your reality.

The *body-mind* is the third critical factor in activating the Law of Attraction. Our physical body has thoughts. (You read that right.) Recently, researchers discovered that heart muscles, the actual cells, have the ability to think. These cells will react before the brain even knows about it. Have you ever heard someone say, "I know it in my gut?" Well, that's because gut muscles are the most simplistic muscles in the body. Often, you know something at a gut level before you do at a mental level. Every cell in the body is a mini brain. You live in a body-mind.

There's a beautiful statement in the Esoteric Golden Dawn Mystery School that states, *"I am the only being in an abyss of darkness, from an abyss of darkness came I forth, ere my birth from the silence of a primal sleep."* **You are the unified field.** You are the reality. So, if in your microcosmic reality, you're not living the life you desire to live and participating in the activities you desire to experiences, then you are responsible for attracting and creating this. One reason is that you are not allowing your imagination to go unchecked and the other reason is that you are still looking for yourself and for the answer. You are still looking for the "try button."

Attraction comes as you pass beyond the "try" stage and into the "doing" stage. The knowing stage must lead to the action stage, where attraction takes place. All of the mystery schools have taught this essential truth: it isn't the magic that makes your life become what you desire it to be. It is NOT about trying, it is about doing. Hermes wrote about this in the ancient scripture accredited to the great god, Tehuti. Jesus talked about it when he said, "What we shall bind on Earth shall be bound in Heaven".

Understand that everyone and everything is a part of you; change YOU on the inside and it begins to change on the outside. Your thoughts attract what you are. Gospel singer, Matthew Ward explained it when he said "As I attract the way, I will travel it." **I'm not just attracting a path, I AM the path. I become the path, I become the way, and I become what I AM.** I like that understanding of our reality because it relates to a whole concept of changing yourself from the inside out and then getting what you desire from the outside in. We don't attract what we desire; we attract who we are.

I like the example from the book, <u>Rich Dad, Poor Dad</u>, in which Robert Kiyosaki discusses wealth. "Being rich" is not about how much money you have. It is about a state of mind; an inner concept or an inner belief system. If that's true, and I believe that is true, my concept is this: you can have as much external money as you want if you can change the internal concept. That's true with any other area of your life as well. The Dad deals with this whole concept of poverty, that rich people – people who are truly rich on the inside – are taught. They live beyond the state of fear. They aren't afraid to go bankrupt because they know they can create wealth again. They aren't afraid to try new activities because they live beyond these limiting beliefs. You don't need that strangulation anymore. You need to act boldly and go in any direction you choose to go.

Whatever is going on in your mind is what you are attracting. When you begin to think and feel love, you can expect more love in your life – not only from yourself but also from everybody around you. That is a guarantee. Begin to think and feel happiness to manifest feeling happy more often. Begin to think and feel like a rich person – and if you don't know what it feels like to be rich, get some books and find out! Find out why Walt Disney wasn't scared of filing bankruptcy before he struck it big with Disney World. Begin to think and feel fulfilled. Begin to think, feel and expect miracles beyond your wildest dreams. Wallace Wattles once said in <u>The Science of Getting Rich</u>, "The more clear and definite you make your picture and the more you dwell upon it, bringing out all its delightful details, the stronger your desire will be; and the stronger your desire, the easier it will be to hold your mind fixed upon the picture of what you desire." Get the book, The Science of Getting Rich. It's a must-read for anyone interested in improving his or her life with the Law of Attraction. Put your mind, heart and passion into your new reality. Macgregor Mathers, founder of the Golden Dawn, said, "Believe that thou art there and thou art."

In other words, you need to believe that you are where you desire to be before you get there. Believe it, not just mentally, but emotionally and passionately. Create pictures and sounds. What does it feel like? What is the movement? Involve as much information as you possibly can to attract your dreams.

Note: Rachael Zink and I have created an extraordinary program designed to aid you in activating your imagination as you creatively visualize. This program "Creative Visualization" is available for instant download at www.lawofattractionsolutions.com.

CHAPTER 2: SEVEN LAW OF ATTRACTION SECRETS

"Those who are certain of the outcome

can afford to wait,

and wait without anxiety."

A Course in Miracles

"Freedom is all in your mind." What an inspirational line from the song "Jericho" by Apollo Craven! This song is a call to action to change your thoughts, overcome obstacles and free your mind. In fact, most of Apollo Craven's songs are designed to inspire you. It's the kind of music that people who are really into positive achieving and the Law of Attraction are going to want to listen to. Do you want the kind of freedom that the Law of Attraction can bring you?

Freedom is all in your mind. There are seven powerful secrets that you can apply right now to change your thoughts so that you start achieving and living the kind of life you desire. These seven secrets are very powerful and important in the process of freeing your mind to open it to magnetic attraction.

The first secret deals directly with your mind. *It is controlling your mind and your thoughts.* That's the secret! If you can't control your mind, who will? In mentoring, people often say, "My husband is always saying this", or "my parents/girlfriend/boyfriend is always saying this." I tell them that maybe they should send their parents, husband, girlfriend or boyfriend to therapy to better themselves! However, we know this is not realistic. You have to take responsibility and control of your own thoughts! That's where your freedom is – it's in your mind and in your thoughts.

Either your thoughts are creating and manifesting the life you desire or they are destroying your dreams. There's no guarantee that life will be easy. Even if you have a foolproof plan, undesirable situations still come up. Sometimes people change their minds or they don't provide what they promised. All kinds of challenges develop in life. You have to be the master of your thinking process. If you control your thoughts, you will control everything else. That's the key.

How do you control your thoughts? You pre-program your mind as you exclaim; "THESE are the thoughts I am going to think." When your thoughts are contrary to the ones you have decided in advance, you recognize them as foreign to you. Then, you shove them aside or dissolve them altogether. It is fundamental to control your own thoughts.

The second secret to free your mind and get the Law of Attraction exploding for you in your life is learning to *control and master your emotions.* This is elementary. If you can't master your emotions, then your emotions are attracting all kinds of experiences; including the situations you never wanted. Keep your emotions focused and in harmony with the kind of lifestyle you desire to manifest. People often say, "Well, I am an emotional person and sometimes my emotions get the best of me." The truth is that **if you**

control your thoughts, you will automatically control your emotions.

On the Kabbalistic Tree of Life, the emanations of the Divine called Hod and Netzach are placed opposite of each other. Hod relates to *thoughts* and Netzach relates to *emotions*. Initiates of the ancient mysteries study the ten emanations on the Tree of Life as a mandala of self mastery. The initiate knows that he or she must master his or her thoughts in order to control his or her emotions.

Let's say, for example, you have a thought that something is bound to go wrong; maybe you're about to go on a job interview. Perhaps you have gone on 200 interviews and nothing has panned out so far. If you think something will go wrong at this interview then you are right. Why are you right? You are right because you are thinking something is going to go wrong but, even more importantly, you are emotionalizing it. You are going into an interview feeling fear, doubt and anxiety. All of these negative emotions are playing into the outcome you are picturing. In order to counteract your fears, you must be open to opportunities. Have a plan and be committed to maintaining flexibility as you follow your plan. Flexibility is a quality that allows you to remain true to your plan even when leads do not become opportunities.

I am currently mentoring a client who is experiencing a lifestyle that is on fire! She filled out application after application without any invitations for interviews but now, she is finally being offered interviews. The interviews are coming because she learned to control her thoughts and emotions. Now, she is on the path to the next level, which is visualizing and emotionalizing her goals.

Visualizing and emotionalizing your goals is the third secret of freeing your mind. It is absolutely essential that you visualize yourself in your new uniform, whatever that may be. It's important to have that visualization of yourself actually participating in whatever you desire. Then, emotionalize the visualization. Feel it and experience it on an emotional level. This is similar to secret two but it goes beyond that into its own secret; it is taking those emotional feelings of secret two and channeling them for the kind of success that you desire.

Visualizing is vitally important. I suggest this method to my clients: if there's something you don't desire, visualize it in black and white; slow it down, make it become a still frame and shrink it in size. The experiences that you do desire, put them in color, put music and sounds to it, put smells to it, put feelings and emotions to the pictures so that you are making them larger than life. While this is a simplistic neurolinguistic technique, it is also a very ancient technique because it's exactly what the mystics used to do with their visualizations or inner journeys.

To summarize, the first three secrets to freeing your mind are: *1) control your mind and your thoughts; 2) control and master your emotions; 3) visualizing and emotionalizing your goals and outcomes.* It is so important to have a plan, see your plan, emotionalize your plan, and run through it in your mind. This doesn't mean it will happen exactly the way you think, but it will be closer to what you expect because you have visualized it several times. What you are doing is practicing the life you desire in your mind.

The fourth secret is *take action now.* Any kind of action is good action. Suppose you have decided what you desire and you're controlling your thoughts. You're putting thoughts in your mind that are in harmony with what you desire and you're mastering your emotions. You are visualizing and emotionalizing your goal. All of this mental work is effective in setting up a winning formula but now you've got to take action. What kind of action should you take? Taking action may be as simple as writing down a phone number, calling someone, and getting some people to do some task to enable you to leverage your actions. You've got to take some kind of an action. Maybe, your first action is hiring a mentor who will help you maximize your attraction potential.

Once a clear decision has been made, you must take action IMMEDIATELY. Don't think of it as something you can do tomorrow or the next day or the day after that – take the action right away. This is part of controlling the overall dynamics of what you attract with the Law of Attraction. Action will get the energy flow of Law of Attraction working for you. **Action shows the Universe you are serious about your goals, so everything can align to make your goals a reality.** Control your thoughts and emotions, visualize and emotionalize your outcomes and then take some kind of action. Start your movement right away and have a plan for more movement.

The fifth secret is to *learn the art of manifestation through specialized knowledge.* I am shocked by the number of people I work with who are going in for a job interview and know nothing about the company. Do your research. I can tell you from my own experience working in the marketing and broadcasting industry, specialized knowledge creates a competitive edge. I never went into an advertising agency or TV/radio station where I didn't know who was managing it, what the format was, what they were doing, and what their goals were. I knew all of that in advance so I was already flowing with the energy of the company. You need to do specialized research to absorb the energy of your goals.

The same is true in having a dynamic relationship. Perhaps communication and interaction in the relationship isn't flowing right now. Maybe your love interest is gone and you desire them back in your life. Start doing research. Learn the kind of energy work that will be effective in transforming the relationship and situation. Learn specialized knowledge in the energy of relationships. Clients frequently tell me they know nothing about energy work and would rather leave that up to me. The truth of the matter is, that human beings, the world we live in and our thoughts are all made up of energy. Understanding how energy works and how it can benefit you is important.

What about getting in physical shape? Everybody has a diet plan. No matter who you talk to, everyone has a plan. There are so many plans out there that you have to do your own research. You are responsible for knowing what will improve your personal health and your vitality. Specialize in knowing how to meet your body's needs and where you are going with your life. It is absolutely essential that you get that specialized knowledge to manifest your dreams.

Suppose you desire to open a restaurant. Do you have the knowledge of the restaurant industry? Even within the restaurant business there are thousands of pieces of specialized knowledge that are part of the restaurant niche, such as food suppliers, kitchen equipment, seating, menu rotation, staffing, etc. Doing the research gives you specialized knowledge which provides you an edge in manifesting the kind of success that you desire.

Learn the secret of manifestation. What is the secret? The secret is specialized knowledge. When you have that information, you can really put together a plan that has a much higher chance of giving you the miracles that you desire. So, control your mind and emotions, visualize and emotionalize your goal, have a plan and follow it, take action now, then learn the secret of manifestation – specialized knowledge is your secret weapon.

Secret six is *work the matrix.* Think of the matrix as a giant spider web. When any part of that spider web is touched even lightly, the entire web is effected and moves. Your thoughts have the same effect on the matrix. Your thoughts and intentions will literally shift everything in the matrix. Everything in the matrix will change, move or alter because you affected the matrix with energy. Remember, everything is energy: actions, thoughts and words are all energy. Take the time to learn how to affect the matrix through energy work. The Matrix can also be affected through a method the ancient teachings call "The Magic of Light." This really is the key.

Walt Disney wasn't just talking about the "Magic Kingdom" when he created his empire; he understood that these thoughts, feelings and ideas could take on physical manifestation. There are specific teachings and secrets that will teach you how to affect this matrix in a magical way. I recommend that you visit or your local bookstore or Amazon and purchase a book called, <u>The Kyballion</u> by The Three Initiates. It describes the seven laws that relate to controlling the matrix. The book is a fairly short easy read. Once you read this book, you'll be shocked at how much impact you can have by following the Law of Vibration and the Law of Cause and Effect. It's an absolutely masterful book.

The last but not the least secret is *love*. Don't be too hard on yourself! You're not too old; you're not too young; you're not too bald; and you're not too skinny! You're the right person at the right time in the right place for your dreams. So, love yourself. REALLY love yourself. Be happy with who you are and love the people around you.

What is the key to love? The key is to stop criticizing yourself. Nothing good, positive or extraordinary comes from criticizing yourself or the people around you. You have extraordinary power and extraordinary gifts. There's nothing you can't do or accomplish in your life. However, as long as you are criticizing yourself, hard on yourself and hard on the people around you, you're taking yourself to a negative state. I've never seen someone in a state of criticism (whether they are receiving or giving) that maintained a positive state of mind.

It is *crucial* to be in a positive state of mind to love yourself. I want you to try this: think of something you can do for yourself every day. It doesn't have to be a big thing; it can be a simple thing. You might choose to learn more about the matrix. You might spend time developing your innate powers. You could take a tour, go through a museum, or visit some place you might desire to work some day. Enjoy an extra-long bath instead of a shower, where you can just meditate allowing all the muscles in your body to relax. You might even visit a spa for a 30-minute massage. There is all kinds of action you can take to love yourself. You don't need massive amounts of wealth to spoil yourself. Find and create ways to feel good about yourself again. Start loving yourself in a very positive way. Then, love the people around you and create an environment of joy, happiness, positive energy and love. That's what forges winners and creates miracles in the Universe.

Let's review the seven secrets:

1. **Control your thoughts; control your mind** – This is absolutely essential because everything starts as a thought. Think about that. Even the Universe itself began in the mind of God. Everything begins with a thought so why not control the thoughts you think? If you don't control them, who will?

2. **Control and master your emotions** – Mastering your emotions is not suppressing your emotions. Master your emotions is utilizing your emotions to create your desires. Take control of your thoughts to master your emotions. Go back to step one and step two will automatically fall into place.

3. **Visualize and emotionalize** – Make those dreams come to life in your mind. See them larger than life.

4. **Take action now** – Three little words: DO IT NOW. There is always a step you can take in the direction of your dream.

5. **Secrets of manifestation through specialized knowledge** – Study the details of how to manifest your deepest desires. Absorb the energy of your desires as you study.

6. **Start taking more control of the matrix** – Get the Law of Attraction working for you. I recommended the book called "The Kyballion" by The Three Initiates. You can also do this through Miracle Mentoring and Alchemy Life Coaching.

7. **Love yourself** – Be positive about who you are and stop criticizing. Love yourself and love the people around you. Love your dreams and seize the day - Carpe Diem. The day is yours. This is your time. This is the place. Make it happen!

Chapter 3: Money, Love, Health, Happiness

"My life is my message."

Mahatma Gandhi

I was watching an episode of Nova last night on "String Theory". String theory deals with the fabric and foundation of the Universe and the magnetism that it has. Scientists are still studying and gathering information on String Theory. However, we know as practitioners of the Law of Attraction and the Magic of Light, that there is an invisible energy that you can attract. This energy can manifest miracles in your life, or it can destroy the structure of your life, depending on what you are actively attracting.

Here is the key: *"As above, so below."* This comes from the ancient sage, Hermes Trismegistus in his written work The Emerald Tablet. That statement may seem kind of vague without further study of the phrase. There are various interpretations of *"As above, so below"* and of the entire Emerald Tablet. Personally, I am fond of the interpretation by Sir Isaac Newton as found in the back of the book. What does *"As above, so below,"* mean?

Your dominating thoughts attract the kinds of experiences you have in your life. For example, most of you know if you're in a relationship that breaks up, deep down you realize that something was wrong before that break up took place. I am often shocked at the number of people that say they had no idea their relationship was in trouble. Most of you know at a gut level that you attract everything into your life; the good, the bad, and the ugly. For example, if you are constantly getting overlooked for the job that you desire, there is some action or thinking that must be changed to attract the kind of promotion or pay raise you desire. You know deep down that the ideas that you have to build a business or company, whether it is a small one or a large one, are only restricted by your doubts and fears. All these beliefs you know deep down. You don't want to admit it but you absolutely know it.

Imagine what would happen if those fears no longer existed. Imagine what would happen if you were intimately connected with your mate. Imagine what would happen if you took away all the self-esteem issues that plague all different areas of your life. Imagine what would happen if you could attract the perfect human into your life, to give you the love that you crave, need and deserve. Imagine for a moment, that you could literally start thinking new thoughts and lose weight. It isn't about cravings, diets or any of that; it's about the predominant thoughts that enter your mind. Once those thoughts change, everything starts changing for the better.

I'm not saying that there's not work to be done, or that you don't have to put forth effort and energy. I'm saying you can remarkably transform your body just through your thoughts. New research indicates that it's not just the brain that thinks, it's the entire body; right down to the cellular level. How many times have you heard about someone's wife dying and three months later the husband dies of a "broken heart"? The heart is part of the thinking process. The liver, kidneys and all organs are part of the thinking process. The old Western modality that you have a brain and a body as two separate entities no longer exists. You have a BODY-MIND. You have a whole body that thinks. Your body thinks in ways that are connected to your brain but it also has a thinking capacity to itself because it is intimately connected to the thinking mind of the Universe.

It's a little confusing but there has been a great deal of research regarding the body-mind. As a matter of fact, scientist now know that the heart begins to react to a heart attack long before the brain even knows about it. Cells in the heart think differently than brain cells do, but they still think. Your whole body is a thinking process which sends out energy. It is a broadcast station for either living a life full of the pain you don't want or a life full of the pleasure you DO want. The choice is yours.

It's more than just changing your thinking. It is knowing how deep your thinking goes. That's what Miracle Mentoring and Alchemy Life Coaching reveals. **Miracles happen when the brain, the body, the mind and the spirit all start working in harmony with the Universe to attract the life you desire.** When you start manifesting and creating, you become a co-creator with the Divine Source. As co-creator, you have extraordinary abilities to channel Divine Source into whatever area of your life you want to flow.

I like the words of Abraham-Hicks. The teachings of Abraham are a conglomeration, which says, "I can choose to feel better". Think about that statement. You can also choose other experiences as well.

You can make a whole list of choices and literally reshape the foundation of your life. For example, I can choose to be kind, I can choose to be loving, I can choose to tell the truth, I can choose to be loyal, I can choose to get up early, I can choose to be healthy, I can choose to be the right weight, I can choose to be wealthy. The list can go on and on. Create your own list. Your personal list reveals a clear understanding of your power. Now, take that understanding of your power and do something extraordinary with it. Create it into a mantra and literally begin to permeate your brain, your mind and the very fiber of your being. You can do this by just taking one word and eliminating it from the example sentences above. Eliminate the word *CAN* so that it will only read *CHOOSE*. Now the examples read, "I CHOOSE to be loyal", "I CHOOSE to be wealthy" and so on.

These aren't statements you make once; they are statements you make internally for the rest of your life. It won't take the rest of your life to begin attracting a whole different construct of energy; expect it to begin working immediately. Choose whatever is important to you. The first step is saying "I CAN do it," and the second step is writing it down and turning it into an incantation using "I CHOOSE". This is an incredible tool because if you start doing these incantations and you emotionalize them, you will see astonishing results.

Emotionalizing doesn't mean just writing your incantation down and pulling out a card and reading it out loud. It means you visualize it while emotionalizing the end result with all your senses: "I choose to be kind," SEE, FEEL, TASTE that kindness. What does it mean to be kind? What are you teaching and showing with your actions? See yourself being kind. Maybe you are using the affirmation,

"I choose to be loyal". See yourself in a loyal position and see people standing by you because you are loyal. Do these mantras 10, 20, 100 times a day and do them for 21 days minimum. You will, without any effort, notice that you automatically make different decisions. You will crave different activities. You'll enjoy experiences that are very different than before. This is all because you are now living at a higher level of deliberate consciousness, vibration and creation rather than the old way you've been approaching life – on autopilot. Remember, write out the action you CAN take, and then switch the word CAN to CHOOSE.

You deserve all the love, money, happiness, and health that you can manifest for yourself. Choose to become the perfect container for the energy you desire to create in your life. What kind of energy do you desire in your life? Do you desire more love? Then, you have to be a container for the kind of energy that will bring you love.

I mentored a gentleman who had 100 requirements for his future mate. He was very stern and stiff about everything that he desired. While it's good to be well defined, you could tell that this man did not love. He wanted a mate that was going to be almost like a child that followed his every direction and listened to his every word. I told him that it's good to have a clear definition of what you desire, but he wasn't being a container of the kind of energy he truly desired. That is true of so many people; they often become the opposite energy of what they desire.

I often mentor people going through divorce and the first secret they want revealed is how to get the other person to change. I suggest to clients, "Let's work on *you* changing first and then the situation will change automatically." Deep metaphysical principles are used in all my Miracle Mentoring to promote lasting change. Little-by-little clients who incorporate these principles into their lives begin to change. Some clients don't change and guess what happens to their relationship? It ends in divorce. However, some clients who do make this inner change occasionally still get divorced. In this case, divorce can be the freedom for attracting love into their lives in a new mate. They have become the proper container with the proper energy for achieving their goals of love. When true change happens, old energies are removed so the new attraction energy has room to grow.

Some people believe that black magic, or negative energy, has influenced their lives. Magic is real and it's out there. I've been in the magical community for many years and I know magic can affect your life because magic is based on the Law of Attraction. You can't live your life based on the fact that someone is thinking negative thoughts about you. You have to be the magnet of magic for your own life. You are responsible for the direction that you want to travel, where you take your life, the career you have and the experiences that you are passionate about. Remember, when you focus on the good experiences and moving in a positive direction, there is no room for negativity.

Money, love, health and happiness come from your deliberate creative actions. What do you deeply desire to manifest in your life? Have you written about what you desire to manifest in positive ways? I don't know if I can fully articulate this but something wonderful happens magically when you write things down. **So write it down!** "This is what I'm going to create in my life; this is the kind of relationship I choose to have; this is the kind of mate I choose to have; this is the kind of business I am starting." Write it down and then describe it in detail. Describe the positive loving and passionate emotions about your business, career, partner, or whatever you are manifesting in your life. Get a composition notebook so you can physically write. They are inexpensive and are the best investment in the store. You can get them in different colors for different subjects in your life. Maybe you want a green notebook for all your thoughts on money or red for love. When you are thinking about that area of your life, pull out your colored notebook and start writing things down. Don't cheat yourself by using digital technology instead of a physical notebook. There is a special kind of attraction that happens when you see all your goals and desires in your own handwriting.

It's nice to desire to have more love, money, happiness or health. What is your plan for attracting those desires? Your plan must contain some action steps. Nothing really happens until you move into the area of action. Action is what gets energy flowing. It sets a positive energy wave into the Universe that starts attraction, which creates more energy and attraction in your direction. Remember, energy begets more energy. So, action is a very important step, but without writing down specifically what you desire, your goals will usually become vague or just a feeling. Write it down, take action and be a fitting container.

I have a client who called and said, "I have a problem. I'm only attracted to athletic women but they are not attracted to me." I asked him what he was doing to attract a nice skinny woman and he told me he wasn't taking any action. He hadn't been successful at getting what he desired which is why he hired me. I asked him to send me a picture of himself. The picture told a story and I knew right away what was stopping him from achieving his goals. He was close to 400 pounds! His energy was not a fitting container for a skinny woman. I'm not saying it's impossible for him to attract an athletic woman any more than it's impossible to pour gasoline in a hat and use it to fill up your car. It's POSSIBLE, but it's not the optimum way.

This man was not the right container to attract a slender woman. The kind of women he desired would likely be found at a gym, vegetarian restaurant, or health food store. I'm willing to bet 99 times out of 100 that most skinny, health conscious women are not going to be attracted to a man that's close to 400 pounds. So, we set up a plan for him to become a fitting container for his goals. He decided to get a gastric clamp on his stomach and set up a plan to become physically fit. Suddenly he became a whole new person. We still had to get rid of the "fat man mentality" because he still feared that he would be rejected all the time. However, by changing that mentality, he was able to find a beautiful slender woman. Together they became a happy couple with a bright future.

You can create some remarkable accomplishments with your life, but always work to be a fitting container for your goals. If you are starting a business, you better know about your business. I was mentoring one gentleman who seemed to be very excited to get into the restaurant business, but when we talked, I discovered that his knowledge of the restaurant business was very limited. It became obvious that he wasn't a fitting container for success in the restaurant business, so we started a program to help him become a fitting container. The key is to make yourself eligible to be successful in whatever you are working on.

Most people need a mentor. Many people that have been successful can go back to different times in their lives where there was a successful mentor to help. Whether it was a spiritual mentor, physical mentor, or financial mentor, they still go back to their mentor. A mentor is someone who is older, more experienced and brings a different way of thinking. A mentor can be found in a book, TV or radio show, podcast, music or other means. A mentor is anyone that plays a substantial role in changing a person's life. A skilled mentor will turn down the noise of life so you can hear your goals. If you're trying to lose weight, you need a way to turn off the cravings. If you're trying to start a business, you need a way to turn off the fear. If you are seeking love, you need a way to open up your heart and soul to a fantastic loving relationship or bring your existing love back into your life. There's a steady noisy hum going on in most of us and that noise often causes self-sabotaging habits.

There are very successful ways to lower the volume of the noise in your head. There are techniques to stop the counter-intentions from attracting unwanted experiences into your life. A professional mentor can help you with all this and much more. I don't say this because I am a professional mentor; I say it because I know it is the truth. Start with the techniques mentioned in this chapter, and then consider a mentor. Remember, there's nothing you can't acquire or experience. **Everything is available to you.** Open your mind, open your heart, and open your spirit to Divine Source and your true potential. There was a time when you believed you could do anything;

go back to that moment and become that person again. Go back to when you believed that your whole life was ahead of you and you could accomplish anything you desired to do. Eliminate the fear and doubts and establish a plan that will help you put the Law of Attraction to work in your life.

CHAPTER 4: THE INCREDIBLE POWER OF GOALS

"Innovation distinguishes between

a leader and a follower."

Steve Jobs

How do you define the word "goals"? Do you define goals as a daily list of things that you dread finishing? Do you define goals as far off dreams that will only happen someday, if you are lucky? Do you define goals as the motivators of your life that push you forward? In neurolinguistics, the word "goals" is replaced with "outcomes" as a way to give more focus and direction to what is being achieved. What kind of *outcomes* do you desire to see in your life? What do you desire to create for your life, the people you serve in the world, your family, friends and the people who depend on you? Both the words *goals* and *outcomes* are applicable in obtaining the life you desire, but they are often used in different settings. If you're sitting in a business meeting, you will most likely hear the world "goals." If you're talking about a relationship, you will probably use "outcomes." What kind of outcome do you desire? What kind of a home life or social life do you desire? They are interchangeable to a certain extent.

Let's examine how to bring these goals to fruition with the focus on outcomes. One of the secrets of the Law of Attraction is that you attract the dominant thoughts in your mind. If you're focused on failure, that's where you're putting your attention and that's a reason why your outcomes are not manifesting the way you desire them to manifest. The secret to success is to focus on the outcomes you desire. Make the outcome, not the current situation, the dominating thought in your mind.

Several years ago, I was working for a television station that had given me a couple of bad paychecks. A good friend of mine, who has now passed away, was also broke. I asked him how much money he had. He said that he had about 15 dollars. It was funny because that's about all that I had, too. So I told him, "It seems to me that we should start our own company." He said the first thing we needed was a business license. My friend had a full tank of gas so we drove down to the county-city building and got a business license for $28. Between the two of us we had $2 left for some coffee. Back then you could get a cup of coffee for 50 cents, so we got four cups of coffee.

Next, we found a notebook for business goals. This notebook was not *his* book, and it was not *my* book, it was *our* book. We wrote down four or five goals. We made a ladder goal list. A ladder goal list starts by writing the outcome you desire. You then work backwards, writing down the steps to get to your outcome until you write down where you are at the present moment. My friend and I had a full tank of gas, four cups of coffee, and a notebook. We were well on our way! We were creating a marketing and advertising firm even though we had no phone number, no letterhead, and no office. We both had children at home and we needed to get some money fast.

Our first goal was to get $200. We needed cash flow so we could get business cards, letterhead and those types of materials. We decided to take on a sports broadcasting project. We used credit to buy slots of time for advertising during a sporting event that was going to be happening soon. Next, we had to focus on selling that advertising time to reach our $200 outcome. My friend and I ended up with $200 and were able to get business cards, letterhead, more gas in our cars, plus we were able to take some food home to feed the babies.

Our next goal was to have $200 in our pocket at the end of the next day and have enough money to rent an office. The next day, we kept that notebook between us in the car and we were singing and laughing and enjoying the day. We were on a Law of Attraction roll. At the end of that day, we had $200 and an extra $250 for an office. It wasn't much of an office but it worked. Our office was in a little place that did small appliance and water heater repair. The gentleman that ran the place was kind of odd but he gave us an office space and the phone line to use when he wasn't there. NOW we were in business!

On the third day we needed an artist to create physical ads. Not only did we create radio and television ads, but we also constructed print and design work. We found an artist at a studio; he was a recovering alcoholic but he was as honest as the day is long. We gave him a key to the shop and told him to do design without limits and we'd pay him as we went. So, now we had an office, an artist, all the equipment and in one week we were up and running!

I won't go through all the details, but suffice it to say, we didn't stay in the water heater business office very long. Soon we were able to move into a nice building downtown with a dentist office and dance studio for neighbors. We were in that building for about a year. My friend and I kept setting goals in our notebook as we applied the science of success and nothing less to our lives. **We actually operated as if we were already there. We operated as if the outcomes had already been achieved. We talked as if it was a done deal.** We were determined to settle for nothing less than success. This was our mindset.

Next, we desired new word processors and a new office that was lush and prosperous. We sought to acquire a place where clients would be able to come into an office filled with design and advertising ideas. This vision for our new office was a place that showed clients that they were working with professionals that really understood their advertising needs and objectives.

To get this outcome we decided to start a weekly entertainment newspaper. Our goal was to sell the paper in 6 months to a year. To our amazement, we ended up selling the newspaper in just 3 weeks for $5,000. That gave us enough money for our original outcome: the lush new office. Our focused and desired outcomes provided the fuel to open up a lush office space next door to our congressman. The office had bay windows that provided an extraordinary view overlooking Commencement Bay in Tacoma, WA.

We took on a client who specialized in renting luxury desks to business people. Our partnership with him gave us that lush office outcome **even when we did not have the funds for the outcome we sought.** We became his advertising and marketing firm and he supplied us with all the office furniture we needed. We looked like we had just walked off Wall Street; especially being in the building right next to our Congressman. **You never know how the Universe will provide you with the outcome of your goals.** Set your outcome, make your ladder-rung goals and watch the Law of Attraction work through the Universe.

We were in that spot for several years producing radio shows and broadcasts. It was all very successful. My partner and I ended up selling the business pieces at a time as we moved in our separate directions. He had some physical issues he had to work through and I had new areas I wanted to explore. I share this experience with you because it is a perfect example of how the science of success and nothing less works. We were living our outcomes before we ever achieved them.

So, the first point is *"don't think OF your goals, think FROM your goals"*. In other words, what if you already had everything you desired? How would you operate differently? Don't be afraid to take risks. My partner and I took risks. For example, renting all of that radio time on credit was an extreme risk. However, taking action proved to the Universe that we were committed to our goals. We were absolutely determined to achieve our outcomes. Don't think OF your goals; learn to think FROM your goals.

My second point is *"give your goals details"*. In other words, what do your goals look like? What do they feel like? What is the color? What does it taste like? What are the emotions tied to it? What does it sound like? When my partner and I started our business, we knew these details. Before we even had clients, we had jingles made up and we had art drawn up. We were ready to take on new clients, we were right there with all the resources to meet our client's need! We rose above the competition of some very big, powerful advertising agencies even though we were just getting started. That was because when we walked in to meet a client, it wasn't about just getting another client, it was about fulfilling a goal and living a dream. We knew what the client wanted and we knew that we could deliver. We had already been there in our minds, it was just a matter of getting the client to share the outcome of our vision.

The third point that is important in your goal setting is *"removing your counter-intentions"*. You have conscious goals, but if you don't remove and clear counter-intentions, you will likely not achieve your goals. The outcomes you desire will be stopped because your fears and counter-intentions will be working like a computer program in the background stopping you. You will be stopped from having the life you desire, the relationships you crave, and the money you deserve.

If you have excess emotional baggage inside of you, that is a nonproductive counter-intention which is equally as damaging as fear or any other form of negativity. The emotional baggage comes up when you start to make progress, things are starting to flow and energy is moving in your direction. You take off in the direction of your outcome and emotional baggage pops up. You think, "Oh no, this is what happened before, I've been hurt too many times or failed too many times". Instead, use this proven plan to fail your way to success by writing your goals down. Write those outcomes down. Goals are important. Albert Einstein says, "Tie it to a goal, not people or things." Einstein knew that goals and outcomes stretch far beyond people and things. People and things will often act as conduits for counter-intentions. They will amplify counter-intentions, fears and doubts.

If you have a powerful goal, don't put it on hold! When we started our advertising agency, if we decided to go out for a drink and see some live music at the end of the day, do you think we forgot our goals? Hell NO! Every action we took was about those goals. So, make your goals a part of your life. Give them a life of their own. Define your goals.

What are your physical goals? **Write them down.** Are you at the weight, cardio strength and physical strength you desire? Do you have the body that will allow you to work, focus and function for 14 hours a day? What are your physical goals? **Write them down.**

What are your mental goals? Before I started Miracle Mentoring and Alchemy Life Coaching, I had a goal of reading two books a week. I'm not talking about paperback novels; I'm talking about hard to understand, occult, metaphysical, business, marketing books. I probably have read 50-70% of every book that deals with success mentality on the market. You don't have to read every book cover to cover to empower yourself with new information. You can read just the bits and pieces that give you the information that resonates with you.

I have read books that were written in the 1800's and early 1900's. I have read the ancient text of Hermes and other ancient documents that outline the basics of Hermetic laws. Are you putting enough time into your mental goals? I have a goal right now to become more proficient in social media. So, I put thirty minutes a day into finding out how to master Facebook, LinkedIn and Twitter. I want to master this knowledge.

What about your emotional goals? Have you really sat down and said, "This is what I desire out of my relationship"? Let me share an experience about a man who set up goals for the woman he wanted in his life and he quickly cut out women that did not meet his "deal breakers". One deal breaker was that she couldn't smoke. No matter how attractive a woman was or how easy she was to talk with, if she lit up a cigarette, that was the last date. He was always a gentleman and cordial, but at the end of the date he would let them know he wasn't interested. Do you have a relationship that isn't working right now? What kind of work are you doing to create an atmosphere and energy that will attract the relationship you desire in your life?

Everyone has money goals. Write down your financial goals and your income goals. How much money do you desire to give to charity this year? How much do you desire to help others out? Set charity goals. If you normally give $100 a year, how about you set the goal of giving $1,000 a year. How much more money would you need to earn to remain comfortable while you give that amount to charity? Set that as your outcome and guess what? You will earn it! You will find a way to attract it into your life.

Last but not least, look at your spiritual goals. Are you setting goals to do your daily ritual work? Do you set aside 15 minutes a day for meditation? What about your involvement in a local church, temple, synagogue or other place of worship? You need to have goals. You can't allow this stuff to just be free flowing. Study for 10 minutes every day and then stick to it. These goals are very important.

I want to share a perspective that resonates with me. Many people see somebody homeless or just getting by and think, "That guy is lazy. He doesn't want to work". The reality is, this person can't stay focused on what they want and what they are trying to manifest in their life. Anthony Robbins says, "People are not lazy, they simply have impotent goals; they have goals that do not inspire them". Are your goals inspiring you? I received a phone call the other day from a woman who just didn't know what she desired. In thirty minutes, I told her two things that she absolutely desired. I was able to realize her counter-intentions through what she had currently created in her reality. The current pain that she was in revealed why her life wasn't working for her. I helped her get these counter-intentions into the open so she could uncover her goals and define two things she absolutely did desired in her life. Now, she has something with potency. She can create pictures, incantations and visualize her outcomes.

Look at the outcomes you desire. Create goals that are empowering your future. **Remember, don't think OF your goals, think FROM your goals.** Create a ladder. Give your goals details. Remove your counter-intentions and emotional baggage. Make a list of your physical, mental, emotional, spiritual and financial goals. You have the tools you need. Now take action and see the outcomes of your goals in the NOW.

CHAPTER 5: SEVEN SECRETS TO EMPOWER YOUR LAW OF ATTRACTION ACTION

"Genius is the ability to

receive from the universe."

I Ching

Numerous people I talk to say they've read <u>The Secret</u>, or have been learning about the Law of Attraction and life seems to be going okay for them, but not GREAT! They wonder, "Why am I not running the business I dream of?", "Why is my boyfriend still gone?", "Why am I not attracting the wealth I desire?", "Why is my career stagnant?" or "Why is my health not where I want it to be?" I get emails every single day from people asking, "Why? Why? Why?"

There are various answers, however one of the biggest problems is called **counter-intentions** or **mind viruses**. I am working with a man who wants to attract a nice woman into his life. The problem is that when we talk about the action he needs to take to get out of the "friend zone", he isn't willing to take action. He is scared and nervous of rejection. This counter-intention or mind virus of fear is holding him back. When you have a counter-intention, it is a subconscious attack on your dreams. So, what is a counter-intention or mind virus made of? Generally, they are made of limiting beliefs

40

and fears which cause the Universe to send you more of what you don't desire. That's why you keep wondering, "Why does this stuff always happen to me?" It happens because you attract it on a subconscious level!

The second biggest problem that can keep you stuck, even if you've written down your goals and created a plan, is that you don't take action. If you don't take action, nothing happens. As a mystic who has studied ancient teachings and the wisdom of Hermes, I deeply understand this. **It isn't a matter of just thinking some way; it's a matter of taking action based on your thinking.** Are you maximizing your potential? Are you maximizing your opportunities? The answer, many times, is no. That is why many aren't getting the Law of Attraction results they desire in life. Let's get into some of the secrets to overcome these problems. They are micro-secrets that make a huge difference. Often times, micro changes in behavior and thought have a massive impact on the life you live.

The first secret is "Guarding your language and using the word *manifesting* instead of want." When you use the word "want," it isn't a bad word in itself, but it denotes lack. The word *want* suggests that you don't have what you desire. On the other hand, the word *manifesting* suggest you are making your desire a reality. Realize that once you manifest your first goal/dream, the second goal will be manifested easier. Millionaires often say that it takes several years to manifest the first million but it only takes two years to manifest the second million and only one year to manifest the third million. Why is that? Think about it. When you have "it", you attract more of what you have. When you don't have it, you attract more of what you don't have. **Like attracts like, money attracts money, and being a loving person attracts loving relationships.**

When you use the word "want", you are communicating to the Universe that you are lacking something. Even more importantly, using "want" communicates to the Inner-verse (the Universe that is inside you) that you are without. I understand that it's not likely that you will be able to completely get rid of the word "want" out of your vocabulary. However, you should start to monitor yourself. Instead of saying, "I want that car," why not say, "You know, I think I'm going to go down and buy that car." You can manifest a $10,000 car or manifest $10,000 towards a new car. I believe you can do that in 30 days or less, in addition to whatever else you earn right now.

It's all about getting rid of the word "want" in your vocabulary and coming up with creative plans or ideas for attracting. There's a trust level there. When you say, "want" it's in the future and you have no control of it. When you say, "I'm manifesting," you may not know all the ways you will manifest it but you do have control over it because you accept that you are a creator. When you get rid of "want", you may not have any idea how you are going to manifest your desire. You just have to know deep down that it will happen because you are attracting it.

The Universe provides untold numbers of resources and ways that your dreams and desires can manifest. What I'd like you to do is write the word "WANT" in big letters on a blank piece of paper. Now, cross out the word "WANT" with a red X. Place this paper in a spot where you will see it regularly for seven days; maybe on the refrigerator or bathroom mirror. This will give you some kind of an outward symbol that you are not going to use that word too much. Obviously there are times when you need to use the word "want" as it's not always a bad word. In the context of manifesting the kind of life that you are capable of manifesting, want is not the best word to express your desires.

The second secret is "the Law of Attraction doesn't just act upon thoughts that you think." In other words, you can think attraction thoughts all day long and nothing's going to happen. The Law of Attraction responds to *vibration* and *feeling*. The Universe does not speak English, it speaks the language of vibration. So, when you expand your vibration and your emotional center until you are absolutely passionate and motivated about what you're going to manifest in your life, that's what the Law of Attraction and the Universe acknowledges.

The Universe acknowledges and responds to the feelings you have towards the goals you are trying to attract and manifest. The higher vibrations that those feelings have in your life, the faster the Universe responds. It's important to stay positive, upbeat and at a high level of vibration towards the goals you are taking action on and manifesting. If you let familiar negative emotions seep in through the back door to feed your fears and apprehensions, the results you seek tend to get canceled out. You end up emotionalizing those fears, not the outcomes of your goals. It's vital to pay very close attention to how your thought process creates an emotional state.

One of the factors that will cancel out anything you are

manifesting, is your fears and anxieties towards being unable to accomplish or acquire your dream. These kinds of mind virus fears and anxieties can overrun all your positive thinking and high vibrational energy. Any unchecked thought can lower your vibrations. Remember what the Law of Attraction responds to: vibrations. It doesn't care if those vibrations are positive or negative. The Law of Attraction is always working. One of the changes created through Miracle Mentoring and Alchemy Life Coaching is a retraining of the mind so fears and anxieties are diminished. This gives the client the power to begin attracting without constant hurdles and roadblocks.

The third secret is "Incantations." If you have studied psychology, it is similar to what is called "self-talk." However, deliberate incantations are more than just self-talk; they are really sitting down and writing up a magically structured sentence about an outcome you are taking action to manifest. Incantations are a direct command to the subconscious mind. Incantations are invoked by repetitive declaration until your subconscious mind absorbs them like a sponge and believes them beyond any shadow of doubt.

For example, a simple incantation is, *"I command my subconscious mind to attract opportunities that make me money every day."* That's a simple incantation. The more that it is said, the more you will see change happening in your life. First, synchronicity will kick in and the Universe will start to provide you with opportunities. Secondly, you begin to see the opportunities and become hyper-aware of them.

I had a client who was looking for "fixer-uppers" that she could get for rock bottom prices, then turn into rentals. She would say to me that there were many opportunities but she was always a week late on finding the deal. So, I formed an incantation which stated that she was always going to be the first to see the opportunities. Quickly, she started finding deals on properties before other people. Why did she get those opportunities? Why did they begin quickly show up? They appeared because she had an emotionalized belief system that they *would* show up. If you have a belief system that something *will* happen, then you have a far better chance to attract a miracle than if you don't believe it.

The fourth secret is, "Writing a manifesting statement". A manifesting statement is a documentation of your goals that you write as if you're living it right now. You should keep it to just a paragraph or a couple paragraphs. It is best written using a computer so you can print out multiple copies. You can also hand write it and make copies. Print out about ten of these manifesting statements and put one at work, one on the coffee pot, one next to your bed, one in your wallet, one on the fridge, one on your dashboard, etc. This statement should be where you can read it ALL THE TIME. A manifesting statement is an absolutely, incredible magical tool of attraction. Magicians have been using this tool for many years and you can use it, too.

So you are probably asking, "How do I write my own manifesting statement?" Here's how it goes:

1. *What am I creating?* Write down what you are trying to create. What am I trying to create in my marriage? – With my boyfriend? – In my career? – With my health? – In my life?

45

2. *Why am I creating it?* Why do you desire this incredible relationship, business, car or other goal? Give the Universe some understanding of why you desire this. Try to make it about yourself, your needs, as well as other people's needs, but also make it esoteric. For example, "I desire an incredible relationship because I have an abundance of love and passion to share," or "I desire to share and help the other person feel that love, light, passion and joy. I know it will not only make us happy but it will also bring positivity to the people around us."

3. This is a very important step. *What happens if I don't?* They say that a bluebird must sing his song or else he will literally die. You have a song to sing, too: whether it's your relationship, your career, or other endeavor, you have a song to sing. This is a very unique song and you have to be able to sing it. In this step, you come to a deep understanding that the pain of not building the life you desire is worse than the fear of going forward. Often people don't move forward because they feel fear, doubt, anxiety or uncertainty about their dreams. I want you to think about and know the gut-wrenching pain you will feel if you don't move forward to the next level with your life. Write out how much pain you will be in. What happens at the end of your life as you look back to see the relationships you didn't rebuild, the business you never started, the health and vitality you could have had? Focus on the pain; not only your pain, but also the pain of the people around you. For example, if you're overweight, how do your children and family feel? It takes a toll on them as well.

4. Finally, make an outcome picture. *What does your desired outcome look like?* When life is going great and couldn't be better; what does that look and feel like? For example, I go to work at 6AM, I'm starting my business, I have clients calling me from all over the world, etc. You want a picture for your mind to settle in on, emotionalize and understand. That's how you apply the science of success and nothing less to work for you. That is how you raise your vibration.

The fifth secret is very simple. It is "accountability". Nobody really wants to hear this one, but being accountable, with no excuses, is critical. How are you using your time, skills and knowledge to take yourself in the direction you intend to travel? How do you activate the Law of Attraction? If you are engaged in an assortment of attraction techniques but you're not taking action, nothing will change. You need to be accountable to yourself. Remember, Law of Attraction precisely responds to action more than anything else. You can designate a notebook to holding yourself honest and accountable. Keep track of actions like; "I stayed in bed a couple hours too long when I could have been up taking action on my dreams." Record the positive action you take to manifest your desires. Notice how action toward your goals causes marvelous changes in your energy field.

The sixth secret is, "Shift your focus from what you don't like to what you DO like." "I do like to make money," or "I do like to see my significant other happy, alive and joyous." Don't focus on all the negative thoughts, focus on the positives. The positive thoughts will push down and funnel out the negative thoughts from your thinking process. Focus on what you do like rather than what you don't like. As you shift your focus to what you like, the Universe starts giving you more of it. That's how it works; that's the whole concept of the Law of Attraction.

The seventh secret is, "Get clear about what you desire!" If you're trying to manifest an outcome in your life because your friends want it, your boyfriend wants it, your boss wants it, it isn't going to work, at least not for any great length of time. Get clear so your emotions can be in line with *your* goals, not *another's* goals. The way to get clear is to seek guidance from a professional Miracle Mentor & Alchemy Life Coach who can help remove your fears, anxieties and blockages in your body – especially if those blockages are in your chakras. You need to remove those blockages so that manifestation energy flows through your body. This is how you become clear about who you are, what you desire, where you're going and how you're going to get there.

If you follow these seven secrets, you are going to make some incredible, astounding progress when it comes to the Law of Attraction. You will be focused on your goals with the emotional support of believing in your dreams. The world is at your fingertips. Take action NOW!

CHAPTER 6: THE UNSTOPPABLE POWER OF "I AM"

"We know what we are,

but not what we may be."

William Shakespeare

Remember when Aladdin rubbed the bottle and the blue genie came out? The genie said, "Your wish is my command." Wouldn't that be exciting to find a genie in a bottle? The Emerald Tablet of Hermes is your genie in a bottle. This tablet teaches the success science of how your wish *truly* is your command. The secret is stated in the phrase **"As above, so below!"** Start creating in the above plane of existence by saying this incantation to yourself a thousand times a day; **"My wish is my command."** What you really desire to build, create and attract into your life is at your command; it's available to you RIGHT NOW. There is not a damn thing stopping you except, perhaps, some counter-intentions. Counter-intentions are like rivers flowing in the wrong direction of the lifestyle you desire.

"My wish is my command." Think about that for a moment. I don't really like the word "wish" because it assumes that your goal is outside of you. Words like "wish" or "want" are dis-empowering because they imply that what you desire is outside of your reality. I understand that we all use these words, including myself. We're all guilty of wishing and wanting but that does little to empower your life. When you say, "I want a new car," what you are really saying is, "a new car is not in my present reality." People that want a new car in their present reality, say, "I AM manifesting a new car. So, I will go look at some cars at the dealerships today." This is a whole different mindset because it says that the new car is within your present reality. You may not have any money for a new car or any idea how you will acquire a new car, but you are making it part of reality instead of a far-off, dreamy wish. It is important to understand that it is within your means to attract your wish. So by saying, "my wish is my command," you're saying you already have all the power and energy you need to manifest your desire. You are accepting and acknowledging that your desires are part your present reality.

The problem with most people is that they don't acknowledge their desires in present time reality. It's always out there somewhere; it's always in tomorrow someplace. If you don't listen to anything else, listen to this: **"The most important time you have for building, attracting and getting what you desire is RIGHT NOW."** There is no time more powerful than right now. Now is the time. It's not next week, next month or next year. Do not live in the future; it rarely comes the way you think it will. People who live in the future are always hoping that tomorrow will be better than today based on taking the same old daily actions. It doesn't work that way.

Taking the same actions and expecting different results is the definition of insanity. If you're using the same mental mind frame with the same actions that you have used over and over and over again while expecting new results, you're not going to get anywhere. Putting action off until tomorrow just doesn't work. The truth is, you're the "Chief of Your Universe" and you can have anything you desire. There's nothing outside your realm when you get into a new mindset. What I usually tell people in Miracle Mentoring is to figure out exactly what they don't want and then invert what they don't want into positive desires. I will be sharing more on this later.

Here's how I like to do this mind-blowing transformational work. It all starts with one of the greatest ancient mysteries of the Law of Attraction. This great mystery revolves around two special words. I will teach you some special incantations using these words. As you study these words and use them on a regular basis, you will see that you are attracting some amazing miracles into your life.

When you begin to formulate your incantations, magnify its effectiveness by using the ancient mysterious phrase, "I AM." This has incredible power because you're actually invoking, in Hebrew, the name of God. It means, I AM presence, I AM gnosis, and I AM now. The most important time in your life is now. "Everything that I AM, I AM now."

Remember the story of Moses? He walks up on Mount Horeb to see a bush burning but not being consumed. Upon investigation, Moses discovers a voice speaking from the bush. When Moses asks the voice its name, the voice says, **"I am that I am."** In metaphysical teachings, it simply means, "I know, that I know, that I know."

Using the power of "I AM" in an incantation shows a deep type of knowing-ness. When your mind reaches that state of knowing-ness, you develop an inner trust between your conscious and subconscious mind. You are then manifesting from a place of harmony within yourself. You become the co-creator of your reality. Understand that your reality isn't what is; it's what you believe about your observations and experiences that make your reality what it is. You have no way of knowing and I have no way of knowing, none of us have a way of knowing what our reality really is. However, we do know that what we believe about our reality determines how we approach our reality and how we act in regards to our reality. If you believe you are too young, too old, too stupid or overqualified, your "reality" will manifest supporting experiences. Situations will arise that reveal you are just who you believe yourself to be.

As I mentioned early, you want to figure out exactly what you don't want and then invert them into a positive "I AM" list. Make a list of 5-10 things you know you don't want. For example, "I don't want to be poor." Now, that's a nasty negative phrase, which makes you think of lack. You shouldn't walk around saying that, but the truth is the majority of people do. Next, you're going to take that phrase and invert it into something like "I AM becoming rich" or "I AM becoming prosperous" or "I AM manifesting wealth daily". Notice the change from the negative "want" to the positive "I AM".

I must share a word of caution as you create your incantation. There are those "I AM" incantations that deal with becoming and there are those that deal with who you are in the present. Here's the problem with some of the incantations written in the present tense. You may say, "I am a billionaire;" but your subconscious mind knows that you are not a billionaire. Your mind is not going to act upon this incantation; you can say it a million times and it's still not going to attract the outcome you desire. Your subconscious mind will believe the saying, "I AM attracting a billion dollar fortune," or "I AM co-creating a billion dollar fortune." I like the word co-creating because you work alongside all the power of the Universe to create through your mind and energy field.

You're co-creating with the Divine Source. You are the instrument of all of Divine Creation; there's nothing you can't create. So if you say, "I AM creating a billion dollar enterprise," that's very reasonable to the Universe. Now start putting your time and energy into making that path open up to you. I see one common theme in the number of biographies of millionaires and billionaires that I have studied. I see that they have a deep understanding how to apply the Law of Attraction through their inner beliefs and incantations. The rich are constantly talking to themselves in present tense as they build their empires. Also, their incantations always revolve around the words, "I AM." I AM creating, I AM building, I AM expanding are all very powerful phrases found in the minds of the wealthy. Even politicians use the magical words "I AM" if they want a career boost. They may say something like, "I am increasing the number of people I am serving." I hope these examples are starting to show you the empowering potential of "I AM".

When you say, "I AM," you're talking about the personal qualities you need to become successful in creating the life you desire. For example, "I AM healthy, I AM active, I AM handsome, I AM attractive, I AM the right age, etc." are quality phrases. When you talk to yourself in quality phrases, your subconscious mind is reprogramming new beliefs about your reality. In other words, you may only have $10.00 in your pocket, but you are becoming a millionaire. When you're talking to yourself with these positive qualities, you will assume those qualities right now even if you believe you don't have them. If you say, "I am gentle and peaceful," even if you have a temper, you are gentle and peaceful. Muhammad Ali repeated to himself "I am the greatest" long before he was the greatest heavy weight champion of his time. You will work these qualities into your subconscious mind. You might see it manifesting as spending less money on coffee or not letting the words of others get under your skin. So change your list of "don't wants" into an "I AM" incantation list. Repeat your "I AM" incantation list to yourself daily; even get crazy repeating them 1000 times a day.

Many people will ask, "Robert, how many times do I have to do this incantation?" My answer is, "Until you're sick of it." Repeat your incantation forwards and backwards, until you are dreaming about it. This is how incantations become embedded in your subconscious mind.

As your "I AM" incantations work their way into your subconscious, you will begin to take on new qualities without even knowing it. For example, "I AM fit, healthy and lean." So, maybe you're a little overweight, but you're doing this incantation a thousand times a day and pretty soon you are certain to notice your appetite going down. There is no magical formula to this; it's the law the ancient mystics taught. It's the teachings of Hermes. It is the power of "I AM." It is the Law of Attraction. Your wish is your command! Your desires must manifest in this world; you're creating in the reality above so it must manifest in reality below.

Your "I AM" phrase seeps into the subconscious by penetrating the metaphysical membrane between your conscious mind and your subconscious mind. The easiest time to penetrate this membrane is those five minutes before you fall asleep. They are absolutely the most vital five minutes of the day to program your subconscious mind to attract what you desire. Make it a habit to use your "I AM" phrases during those five minutes as you fall asleep. The membrane between your conscious and subconscious mind is also easily penetrated during physical activities like exercise and sex.

Perhaps you have somebody you desire to get back into your life that left you, or maybe you are having some negative events happen in your life that you can't explain. Creating an "I AM" incantation to deal with that particular issue will change everything. "I AM in control of my reality; nothing controls my reality but me." I understand that some of you are dealing with some negative forces and harmful energies that may be beyond the normal spectrum of reality. In these cases, start using "I AM" incantations then seek professional assistance. (www.lawofattractionsolutions.com)

The key to the "I AM" incantation is immediate action. You have to begin with some kind of action immediately. Notice how the incantation grows stronger as you apply physical action. For example, I struggled with writing. It was always a task for me to sit down to write; whether it was for a blog, an article, or a book. I have since trained myself as a writer and I enjoy my creation when I get it done. I obtained this level by using "I AM" phrases like, "I AM writing empowering and compelling information for people all over the world" and "I expect people to love what I write." When I have that vision in my mind of people reading my blog or books, when I see them enjoying it and making positive life changes, I am even more motivated to write. When I am writing, I will pause, take a deep breath and say my "I AM" phrases. It is important for you to apply your incantations while you are in the action of what the incantation was created for.

Let me share a secret that will make these incantations even more powerful. The secret is this: there is a significant amount of research that shows an "I AM" phrase formed into a picture or feeling surrounded by emotionalized excitement causes the new belief to be strengthened exponentially. For example, just saying "I AM driving a new Jaguar," is good. It becomes great when you take the action of seeing that Jaguar and feeling yourself behind the wheel. Feel the leather, see the gold trim, smell that new car smell and hear the engine. You need to hear it, feel it, smell it, and see it. If you practice creative visualization along with your "I am" incantation, your desires will soon manifest. Emotionalizing incantations exponentially increases their attraction power.

Here are some clever ways to emotionalize your incantations! When you exercise, use that as your time for empowering your primary incantations. While your heart rate is up and you're sweating, you are in an emotionalized state; the perfect state to empower your incantations. Emotions affect and excite the body just like exercising does. When you're on that treadmill, bike, elliptical or other exercise equipment, that's the time to blast those incantations into your subconscious mind.

Your subconscious mind is your connecting link with the Infinite. The worst force you can have in your subconscious mind is fear. Job 3:25 in the Bible says, "For the thing which I greatly feared is come upon me, and that which I was afraid of is come unto me." Often, we as humans emotionalize paralyzing fear and negativity, thus clouding the subconscious mind. This causes the creation and manifestation of the experiences you do not desire.

There's nothing stopping you from attracting what you desire. You have incredible power. I have worked with people all over the world and I have never met a person who didn't have unlimited potential to attract whatever they desired. I have seen people with unlimited potential write down their goals, plan it all out, but then nothing seems to manifest or work out. This is a common problem with many people. The problem is counter-intentions and mind viruses. Counter-intentions are the little viruses in your brain that are sending you in the direction opposite of what you desire to travel. When counter-intentions are present, the harder you try the worse it gets. The counter-intentions are your subconscious beliefs that say you cannot reach you goals. Perhaps, the counter-intentions are phrases you heard in childhood that you don't even realize are a part of your belief system. For example, "Money doesn't grow on trees," or "You will always have to work hard.", may be a belief you are consciously unaware of.

Dig through your beliefs and self-talk until you have removed and transformed all your counter-intentions. Until all counter-intentions are eradicated, you will constantly attract the opposite of what you truly desire. So, it is vital that you transform all of those counter-intentions. The power of the "I AM" mentality will open the door to your unstoppable energy to create the world you desire to live in. Begin now. Start with "I AM creating the life I desire."

CHAPTER 7: YOU CAN MAKE MIRACLES HAPPEN

"I am realistic –

I expect miracles."

Wayne Dyer

Would you like to become open to receiving miracles? This is the chapter for you! I want to remind you of one truth before we get into the subject of miracles. Remember that everything discussed in this book requires one step: ACTION. Nobody ever achieved greatness with an "everything just happens by chance" attitude. You are either all in or all out; simple as that. There's no half way on this. You cannot just leave everything up to fate. It's disappointing because I have seen and worked with people who have the potential to do incredible wonders with their lives. They are excited and passionate but they fail to take action. **Attraction doesn't work without action.**

Let me give you an example. Andrew Carnegie built a huge empire. He did this by creating a team while employing a very precise interview process. Anyone that went through a Carnegie interview would be informed of all the details about the opportunity. At the end of informing the potential hire, Carnegie would ask, "What do you think about this opportunity, would you like to do this?" If the person took more than thirty seconds to decide, they were immediately disqualified for the open position. Andrew Carnegie only worked with people who could make decisions quickly and take action.

Some people say that it makes sense to think about it for a day or two, but all the evidence points in the other direction. Here's why: if you know what your purpose is, if you know why you're here, if you know precisely what you desire and what you don't desire, if you know beyond any shadow of a doubt, then you know in a heartbeat whether an opportunity fits or doesn't fit into your life. My question to you is, why do you hesitate? Why aren't you taking action? Do what you need to do to perpetuate the Law of Attraction: Take action!

One action you could take is getting started with Miracle Mentoring and Alchemy Life Coaching! Success coaching is a powerful way to leverage your time. You either desire to get to the next level or you don't. Either way, it's fine! The point is you need to be effective and efficient in your thinking. Miracles require you to have a plan, have a destination and a road to travel on. Designing a plan is where the Science of Success and Nothing Less begins. What do you desire to attract? What kind of miracles do you desire to bring into your life? The Universe is so vast, so enormous, that often you will exceed your wildest dreams and expectations. You can go far beyond anything you've ever imagined. You can manifest MIRACLES!

I remember many years ago, I was looking to manifest a job in radio broadcasting. I perceived this job as safe, easy, and enjoyable. At the time, I had a mentor coaching my thinking. As I changed my beliefs, I started attracting miracles. Unexpectedly, I got a call from a

TV station that was pouring millions of dollars into this new channel called Fox. The next thing I know, that TV station in the Seattle-Tacoma market hired me. This experience became a wonderful stepping stone to my next goal of owning my own advertising and marketing company. You never know what the Universe is going to do to expand your outcomes when you have a clear picture of what you desire and where you are going.

Once you have a clear picture, you have the tools you need to actually begin attracting and receiving the miracle that you desire. Even if you have well-defined goals, when you are not open to receiving the miracles that you desire and need, you are being closed to miracles and manifestation. Think about this for a minute. Have you ever been closed to miracles before? Maybe you said "no" to a small door that could have been the stepping-stone to your miracle. This is called "self-sabotage". Everyone is guilty from time to time of self-sabotage to some degree.

Are you looking for an incredible, heart pumping, life stopping relationship? Do you have a boyfriend or girlfriend that has gone a different direction and you have no idea why? Would you like to salvage that relationship and give it vitality and excitement? Have you been passed up for a big promotion, even though you were qualified? Did you miss buying your dream home by a narrow margin? If you answered, "yes" to any of these questions, you have not created yourself to be a fitting container for the miracle you seek. Ask yourself, "Am I opening myself up to receive?" Have you been thinking about starting a new business for the past 2, 3, 5, 10 years? The first step after you have an idea of what you desire is to become a fitting container to receive the miracle of your dreams and desires.

Let me give you an example. When it comes to personal relationships and helping people find the love of their life, it's easier than you think! In my many years of Miracle Mentoring and Alchemy Life Coaching, when I talk to men who desire a relationship with a special woman they say they're excited and motivated to meet "the one". However, when I ask them when was the last time they brushed their teeth, trimmed their toenails, etc, you would be shocked at the ridiculous answers I get to this second question. If you're overweight, have a haircut from the 1930s, your clothes are worn, you are unemployed and pawning your belongings, then you are not a fitting container to receive the miracle of a beautiful, special relationship. All of these qualities keep you from attracting what you desire.

Here's the argument: "Well, I've got to tell you that I just desire a woman that's going to like me for who I am." Believe me, you can be WHOEVER you want to be! You don't need to be a slob. I do not believe that is who you really are. Remember, whomever you choose to be, you will also attract the like. Likes attract likes. You're not limited by your environment, upbringing, or culture. You have the power to change it all and become a container for your miracle. The same situations is true for women. There is a man who wants to give you an incredible relationship, you just have to be a fitting container. If you desire a tall, dark, handsome, muscle man, then it is time to quit sulking on the couch with a tub of ice cream. Get up, go for a run, and transform yourself into a container for a muscle man. **It's important to know how to create yourself into a container for anything you desire to attract.**

Here is another example of becoming a fitting container for a miracle. If you were applying for a high paying office or lawyer position, how would you dress? You certainly would not go to the interview in your flip-flops and Hawaiian shirt. You would not lean back and put your feet on the desk during the interview. You would be a fitting container. You would wear a nice suit, shake hands, remember names, and send a thank you note for the interview. It often comes down to making yourself a container for your miracle.

Part of transforming yourself into container for your miracle is developing a miracle mindset. Do you have positive expectations? Are you seeing positive outcomes regarding your career, love, body, and abundance building? If you're sitting there thinking your desires probably won't manifest, then you will not attract the miracle you seek. At some point you have to take some action in your physical and mental life. Let the Universe know what your intention is. Let Divine Source recognize who you are creating yourself to be. You must set your intentions then let go and trust the Universe! **Let Divine Source, God, the Universe, Mother Nature or whomever/whatever you call upon, take over and manifest your miracles for you!** Stay positive expecting your miracle to come to you. Don't choke your miracle with doubt, worry, or fear. Express your intentions, stay in a positive mind frame, LET GO and watch the Universe align a miracle or two for you.

You've heard the old saying, "I'll believe it when I see it." Unfortunately, it doesn't work that way. People who create miracles are visionaries who see it *BECAUSE* they believe it. This is one of my favorite sayings: "Unless you believe it you're likely not going to see

63

it". If you don't believe that you can walk across the street and check your mail, you can't. I have seen people isolated in their own home, unable to walk across the street because they didn't believe they could.

In order to attract the miracles you desire, in order to be open to receive these gifts, it is important to expand your belief system. Small belief systems get small gifts and miracles. A big belief system gets big miracles, and an unlimited belief system gets unlimited miracles! There have been many people in life who have had incredible wonders happen to them just because they were open to believing in it and receiving it!

What can you do to become more open to the kind of miracles you desire? You can create an inventory of all the beliefs that limit you. Write down a few places where you feel limited, then write some positive beliefs and incantations, which you can use to begin to feed into your subconscious mind. If you're going to write a belief expansion incantation, you don't just read it once, you say it over and over, until it becomes a passionate part of your life. Unless you create it to be passionate, it won't migrate into your subconscious or unconscious mind. Once your belief expansion incantations are in your subconscious, it will begin to work for you. You will see miracles when you begin to believe they *can* and *will* happen!

As Og Mandino wrote in the Greatest Sales Man of the World, **"I am nature's greatest miracle."** Therefore, if you are nature's greatest miracle, creating miracles should be second nature to you. Miracles begin with belief and expectation. "Today, I will manifest a miracle."

Chapter 8: More Love, Love, Love

"Life is too deep for words,

so don't try to describe it,

just live it."

C. S. Lewis

At the end of the day, I have never heard of anyone laying on their deathbed wishing they had spent more time in the office. No. Instead, they wish they had spent more time with family and friends. They wish they had loved more. **Nobody ever regrets loving.** There is never regret when people sacrifice their life for love.

Will you come to a deep understanding of the truth in your life? Will you live an authentic life with the understanding that you are a spiritual being having a human experience? Will you fulfill your central mission, which is to LOVE? If you answered yes to these three questions, you are traveling in the direction to attract the love you crave.

Many people go through life lonely. You can see them in the store or at the mall; they are hunched over, looking down, they have not smiled in a long time, and they look almost gray. These people are filled with an interior loneliness because they haven't experienced the incredible pleasure and joy of love. **Love is the ultimate magic in the Universe.** Your thoughts can greatly affect the love you attract in your life. If you're afraid of losing something, you're operating out of fear and you're not likely to attract love. However, if you're excited about becoming someone special, then love is the ultimate medicine; there is nothing that compares with it in the Universe. Love is eternal. Love is transformational. Love is alchemical. Love is magical. Love is all of these things plus much more.

American novelist, Stephen Chbosky says, "We accept the love we think we deserve." There are so many people in the world today who are accepting less than complete and total love. When they don't get true love from their mate, they try to retrain their mate or seek affection elsewhere. If somebody naturally, on their own, doesn't want to pour their heart, soul, and spirit into you, you can't retrain them to do so. However, you can show them what will bring joy into your life and learn what brings joy into their life.

We live in a time when many people say, "I don't know about love, I just want to have some good sex, or make some money and be happy." People are constantly looking away from the one thing that will give them everything else that they need: LOVE. They accept less than they deserve because they believe at some level that they don't deserve very much. Again, Stephen is right: "We accept the love we *think* we deserve."

If you desire to begin to change your thinking right now, say this powerful affirmation, **"I deserve an incredible amount of love in my life. I deserve to be loved beyond anything I've ever felt or experienced. I am open to being loved all the time, 24/7."** This might have been hard for many of you to say. Keep saying this affirmation and you will begin to believe that you deserve to be loved. As your beliefs about love begin to change, say **"I deserve love because I am willing to give love in return. I am willing to pour my heart, soul, spirit and actions into another person."** If you think about your significant other as you say this, you will begin to realize a startling improvement in your relationship.

To attract more love into your life, expect to be completely and totally loved. Settle for nothing less. When your expectations are focused on the love that you can bring into your life and you affirm that in your mind, you will find that the love you desire begins to blossom. Notice how other people reduce love to just a sound bite; just a phrase that we end the conversation with or another way of saying goodbye. Is that the kind of love, joy, happiness and fulfillment that you desire in your life? Have you reduced your love to a sound bite or a way to close conversations? Open up to the true potential of love and expect to be completely loved.

True love is not an illusion. It is magic that is manifested. A large portion of the population today have reduced love to the point that they don't even desire to talk about love. They will talk about anything else but love. True love is where everything comes together. Take a magician and put him into a sanctuary where he is doing magic and notice how the magician conforms reality to his will. He uses the Law of Attraction to manifest wonders. However, take away the love and passion and the magician's magic dies without manifestation. **Without love there is no magic.**

Love is like the person who is passionate about life and their work. They always get up early with enthusiasm and excitement for a new day. I'm thinking of W. Clement Stone who would get up at 3:00 A.M. He couldn't sleep because he was so passionate about what he was doing with his company. You can have that passion too. It's not just about love with another person; it's about loving every part of your life. Why do you love your work but not your mate or vice versa? The Law of Attraction is always working; especially in the area of love and passion. The Law of Attraction is an incredible tool that will allow you to attract anything you desire into your life. **It's easy to manifest love into your reality.** More importantly, you can manifest the relationship you desire into your life; a true loving bond with another, not an illusion.

Pay attention to what I am going to advise. I know you're focused on your work, exercise program, social life, paying bills and so on. You're focused on the many (and sometimes overwhelming) experiences and responsibilities of life. I am here to tell you that if you desire to attract true love beyond your wildest dreams, you better **make love your first and last priority.** Love should be your first thought in the morning and your last thought at night. Love must be constantly rolling through the back of your mind all day long. "How can I express my love? How can I complete my love? How can I share my love?" You don't have to wait for Christmas to give your love a gift. You don't have to wait for the marriage to be falling apart to get her some flowers. Love is about spoiling each other and making each other feel incredible. When referring to love in the workplace, love is about the passion and joy that makes your employees and customers feel important, special, cared about and, of course, LOVED.

I can hear you exclaiming, "I really love this woman and I show her all the time, but she doesn't love me back." In this case, the circuit of love has yet to be connected. Love is a circuit; it is the circuit of "I give, I receive, I give, I receive". Some people say, "Isn't it wrong to give to receive?" Absolutely not. Let me explain.

You give in order to have room to receive. You receive in order that you might have something to give. It becomes a circuit, back and forth and it never stops; it always grows and multiplies. If you always gave without receiving, there would come a point where there would be nothing to give. If you always received without giving, there would come a point where all that you received would smother you.

If you desire to love completely, you must invoke the Law of Attraction to pave a path for the creation of a circuit of love with the one you adore. Until the one you love desires to love you back completely and fully, you have no way to love them totally. Remember, love is a circuit that can be enhanced with the Law of Attraction.

I met an elderly couple many years ago in the Caribbean. They were walking naked on the beach together. I had lunch with them and they said, "Even though our bodies have slowed down a bit since we were in our thirties, our love is just as strong today, if not stronger, than it was then because we've been multiplying it." Love created by the Creator grows stronger. The new part is the first spike in the ground. If you're doing it right, passing the energy on and making the person you love feel incredible amounts of love and they're giving it back to you, you've just begun. The newness of falling in love doesn't wear off, it gets stronger. **True love is always becoming more powerful.**

Do you really desire to have the love you crave in your life? Are you tired of bouncing from one mate to another? The new social trend in this country seems to be "serial monogamy". It used to be that people got together and were monogamous; even if there were problems in the marriage. Today, what we have is not even real monogamy. Monogamy is when two wolves mate together and stay together their whole lives. Even if one dies ,the other wolf hardly ever finds another mate. That's real monogamy. What we have is serial monogamy. Your monogamy might be good for 6 months, a year, two years or ten years. That certificate of marriage that you cherish so much is a worthless piece of paper. The truth is, there are so many people having a relationship outside of their monogamous marriage that it somehow seems normal. I want you to be real, authentic and true with yourself. I want your heart to be full of incredible amounts of joy and love. It's not about a certificate; it's about sending love out and receiving love back.

Society has become cynical. People are into everything but true love. People love things that do not love back, that can't complete the circuit of love. We love coffee, we love shoes, we love movies, we love cars, we love music but we do not love each other. However, if you believe in love, you're going to attract it. If you still believe in that spark of light that is beyond recognition, beyond definition and beyond anything you can imagine; if you believe in that spark of light that comes from God; if you're truly committed to that spark of light and believe in it, then YOU WILL ATTRACT LOVE.

When you find that spark of light, that incredible love or when the door of love opens to you, then you better walk through because the door doesn't stay open indefinitely. Love is energy and energy is never stagnant. It needs to be grounded to flow in a circuit. So when the door opens to incredible love and light, be ready to dance through that door.

I have seen the door of love open to many people. Many have had a chance to experience love beyond anything that they have ever experienced before; a partnership, friendship and deep communion with someone. Many have had a chance to love but don't walk through love's door. I am not a person who regrets, but I know that those who hesitate to walk through the door of love regret it when the door closes. Don't let any fear, doubt, opinion, or belief hold you back from completing a circuit of love. People who believe in love find love because they desire it, see it, and believe it. This is the power of creative visualization. This is the power of the Law of Attraction.

Be advised: do not confuse your habits, your marriage, or your relationship with love. A habit is not love. Just because you can't break the habit doesn't mean you're having a love affair. A love affair is passionate, growing, blossoming and it takes you to new heights and places you haven't been before. Let me say this: marriage and love have very little to do with each other. Unfortunately, marriage is a business arrangement in our society. It's sad but that's the way it is. Do not confuse your habit of being married with love. Love builds the other to be the best they can be. A habit is just being stuck in the some routine.

Keep this in mind: you can do anything you desire in life. There's nothing you can't do. There are no boundaries to love. I'm thinking about King Edward. Here's a man who was King of the British Monarchy in the 1930's. He fell head over heels in love with an American woman. King Edward fell so passionately in love that he gave up the throne of England to be with the woman he loved. He never regretted it, he never looked back, and he never stopped building the circuit of love. His brother, who took over the throne, made him a Windsor and eventually King Edward had to leave England for good. He did that for love. You can have that type of love too. Why settle for anything less when you can invoke the power of the Law of Attraction to bring the person you love into your life? "I am attracting love because I am giving love."

CHAPTER 9: HOW TO SAVE YOUR RELATIONSHIP

"Lord, make me an

instrument of Thy peace."

St. Francis of Assisi

I am dismayed to see that relationships are falling apart at a record pace. Of course, there are relationships that might do well under a different set of circumstances or if the rules of the game were changed. Failing relationships can also be blamed on the Law of Attraction not being invoked by everyone in the relationship. Whatever blame you may place on a failing relationship, changes can be made to rescue and recreate that relationship into the most loving experience of your life.

All too often, one person or the other will call and ask for help because their significant other has taken off "out of the blue". In Miracle Mentoring and Alchemy Life Coaching, clients learn to invoke the Law of Attraction while using Miracle Magic to change the entire energy of the relationship. It's important to have your mind in the right place to rescue love. Sometimes, you even need someone to guide you. Even if you have a great and rewarding relationship, it's important to read this chapter. The information in this chapter can teach you to enhance your love in many different and powerful ways.

Do you know how to apply the Law of Attraction to

relationships? Can you use the Law of Attraction to drastically change your life? Can you rescue the love you once felt? Of course you CAN. The Law of Attraction applies to every aspect of your life from your health, friendships, relationships, work, business, and home. In fact, it applies to everything. We are co-creators with Divine Source, The Universe, and/or God. The Law of Attraction is the most powerful law in the Universe.

I believe in your ability to use free will. You are a co-creator of your microcosm. You can create to whatever level your free will is expressed in your life and your reality. You have the power to create the reality you desire. You can see examples of this all the time. People come out of concentration camps or prison and create extraordinary lives. *If they can do it, SO CAN YOU.* The same is true with your relationships. **You can create an extraordinary relationship.** You have the power to do more than just rescue a broken relationship.

Let me share a few keys to rescuing a relationship with you. If you've had relationships before that have gone sour, ask yourself "what are you going to do differently this time?" What will you do different this time to make sure it doesn't happen again? You have to be tapped into who you really are and what your potential is. Is your potential more than just a 6 or 9 month fling? Are you living up to your potential when it comes to developing and building a powerful and loving relationship? If you are not living up to your relationship potential, the Law of Attraction gives you an opportunity to change yourself from the inside out. Isn't that important?

Think about it. You have the ability to not only change the world around you but, even more importantly, you have the ability to change yourself from the inside out. I think that's incredibly important. When you realize that you can change who you are, then love can become your reality. As you start making changes, you start vibrating at a different frequency. It's like you found a key that starts opening up locks that you couldn't open before. You've changed yourself from the inside out.

Remember, I am talking about not taking the same old repetitive action in the same old repetitive way. It's not just about discovering yourself. Forget about finding yourself! You are not lost so there is no need to discover or find yourself. **You are simply what you choose to create.** GO create yourself. Take different action and change your thought patterns. BE who you desire to become. Define *"you"* in advance, before love. Know how you will create your life through the different choices you will make.

The same is true with your relationship. What do you desire your relationship to be? In other words, if your girlfriend said she can't take it anymore and she walked out the door, it's no longer a matter of patching up the same old relationship. That might work for 6 months or a year, but in the long run, it's not going to be effective because you have not changed. You're still at the same vibratory level and she's in the same mind frame so nothing has changed.

Some people say: "But he won't change so why should I?" Understand, you're *not* changing for him. You're changing *for yourself.* If you change for someone else, that's not a full, complete change. Before you make any change in yourself, there must be a personal commitment to embracing the benefits of that change. Are you getting something out of the change? If you are, then it makes sense to do it for yourself. Learn how to take different action as you choose to design yourself. Prevent another dead end relationship in the choices you make about the reality you create.

Many people use the Law of Attraction, but when enhancing your love attraction you must also use the Law of Similarities. Law of Similarities is akin to a neurolinguistic technique called "mirroring". In the beginning of your relationship, you had a rapport with your lover. You saw only the best and brightest in each other. In the beginning you focused on your similarities. After a time, your focus shifted from your similarities to your differences. When people are focused on their differences, the inevitable is likely to happen; a break up or an unhappy relationship.

When you change yourself, you say, "I want to decide what I REALLY am. My decisions not only effect myself but also my relationships because my vibrational energy is shifting." If you are steadfast in these positive changes and you are really determined to live them, then, as you begin to shift, your partner will also begin to shift. It doesn't even matter if he or she is nearby. **The invisible connection in the universe will provide the conduit for the change.** What happens is your lover will start to subconsciously mirror you.

For example: if you give your partner the iron fist, then that's what you will get back. That's what relationships are about; they're about ebb and flow of energy between two people. You need someone

76

who is open, honest, loving and caring and desires to work with you in the energy currents of the relationship. That's what the Law of Attraction is about. It's a matter of what you decide you desire to attract. What energy do you desire to create in your own microcosm that will be reflected back through the Law of Similarities? Remember that the Law of Similarities comes after you define what you are going to do different in this relationship. Defining who you are, what you desire to be and your intention is first and foremost. What is it that you desire to be? It's not who you are, it's what you desire to be. Write down those intentions and start taking action so that you are living at a new vibration.

The next part of rescuing a relationship is defining the details of your relationship a more specifically. Define what was or currently is rocking your relationship boat right now. Ask yourself these three questions, "What was my relationship? What is my relationship? What can my relationship become?" Write it out and define it, word for word: "I believe this relationship has the power/potential to be…" Write it in clear words. For example, "My lover is the kind of mate that works with me to see all our mutual and individual dreams fulfilled." Define those dreams. Then, create a picture in your mind to go along with it. What are these dreams? Do you dream of building a business or do you dream of traveling the world? In a true loving relationship, you have this massive creative ability to execute all your dreams, all the time with both your creative minds. Remember the Law of Attraction does not speak English; it speaks vibration which is created through visualization. (To obtain our Creative Visualization Program visit www.lawofattractionsolutions.com)

As with the Law of Similarities, don't wait for your lover to start dreaming or changing. You should be visualizing your perfect relationship all the time. Don't visualize it and then get discouraged when you don't see it manifest overnight. Visualize it and stay with it. Create a vision with so much energy that your lover is enveloped in the dream you are dreaming.

Slowly begin to share the vision with your lover. You might share it by saying something's like, "Wouldn't it be nice if...", or "Couldn't we possibly do this...", or "Doesn't it make sense to live like this..." Now, watch and see where it goes. See where you need to bring your lover's response into harmony with your visualization. **Your creative visualizations will change your love life exponentially so practice creative visualization often.**

You can change the very context of your relationship. It takes some strong visualization and a little less dogma. Ask yourself, "Can my lover feel the love or energy of the dreams I desire him or her to experience? Is my love and desire strong enough within me that it overflows into my lover?" Perhaps you need to focus on intensifying your love and passion. Or maybe it is time to move on. Not every relationship is worth saving. Some relationships were good at the start, but they have run their course and served their time. This generally happens when one partner is growing in a different direction. When relationships end it is usually because, at some point, people stop talking and their individual and mutual dreams change.

Maybe there's a chance that you could create independent lives within the relationship but still live under the same roof. Are you open to that idea? Somehow just having a roommate doesn't make sense when you could create the love of your life with a mutual dreaming partner. Some relationships are just not worth hanging on to and you have to define that for yourself. Use the tools of creative visualization to assist in defining the details of your relationship.

Here's a quality that really tears relationships apart: FEAR. People start looking at their life and they think, "Oh my God! Am I going to be in this loveless relationship my entire life?" Unhappiness causes people to look at their desires for their entire life. We're human beings. We all look at that and then fear starts popping up. When fear outweighs positive feelings, the relationship has run its course unless you and your partner challenge your fears. There are more fears than the fear of being unloved; there are also money fears and fears about different values and beliefs.

You need to understand that fear will destroy your relationship faster than anything else. What you absolutely must do is create an environment where your lover feels safe. If either of you in the relationship are living in a state of fear, then fear is what you are attracting through the Law of Attraction. All of that fear becomes a dark cloud in your relationship. The fear even ends up in your bed. A relationship cannot be maintained in a state of health while being in a state of fear. If you're in a state of fear about always doing or saying the wrong thing, something's wrong with that relationship. **Fear must be eradicated in that relationship or that fear will destroy your relationship.**

Fear is one of the most damaging acids you can pour on a

relationship. Miracle Mentoring clients experience my skill at immediately revealing the core of the fear that is disempowering the relationship. This is also the skill you need to develop as a partner in a relationship: you need to disempower your partner's fears. One way to disempower fears is to express your own fears with your lover. If you can't express your fear openly and honestly, then you've got some serious problems that need to be taken care of. Relationships are made to work as a team. Each team member must communicate with the other to accomplish lasting love.

Let's say the two of you get together and you both desire miracles in your life. You're both invoking the Law of Attraction and you're writing your outcomes down as they relate to your relationship. The two of you have decided to have the most loving, incredible, expressive, successful, sexually fulfilling relationship that you've ever had in your entire life. You agree that you desire your love to get stronger as time goes by. You agree that you desire to be nurturing to each other and those around you, so that everywhere you go people are affected by your enormous love.

Let's say you both like that outcome; it feels good, it feels right. Once you have decided as a couple what you desire from the relationship, you must begin digging up all counter-intentions! **Counter-intentions are self-sabotaging thoughts or fears and anxieties that live within your subconscious mind.** Most counter-intentions come out to shine at the worst and inappropriate times. These counter-intentions can keep you from having the incredible juicy love that the two of you really desire. Each of you may have your own set of counter-intentions along with mutual couple counter-intentions. It's very important to find out what those are so that fear does not hinder love.

If the two of you are split up right now, specially designed energy work, like Miracle Magic, can get the two of you back together. The first question I ask is, "What are your counter-intentions?" Your positive intention is to make a loving environment for the two of you, but what are you doing to sabotage yourself? It's important to dig deep to find your true counter-intentions. **There is absolutely nothing worse than self-sabotage.**

Self-sabotage is seen all the time in business. Entrepreneurs who are taking the correct actions and increasing their wealth then they begin to fear success thus sabotaging themselves. The same experience happens in relationships. Have you ever wondered why couples create a wonderful joyful first seven years, then all of a sudden the relationship make a turn for the worse? A lot of times, certain life indicators take place and they awaken old fears and counter-intentions. Once the counter-intentions start going full speed, it is like a merry-go-round, which can only be stopped with a **MIRACLE.** This miracle can be manifested through the positive pictures you create in your mind and the invocation of the Law of Attraction. BEWARE: These counter-intentions, memes or mind viruses aren't just from your own thoughts; sometimes they're from family, friends, business partners, etc. They'll make little statements like, "Joe is a nice guy, but I think you could do better." Those statements get into your subconscious mind, ripping it apart from the inside out. I really believe when people make those statements, they know what they're doing. They are putting their desires for your life into your mind. If you've had people plant negative seeds about your current relationship, you need to extract those seeds before the seeds grow into weeds that choke the life out of your love and relationship.

Once you have discovered what your intentions are and you have uncovered a list of counter-intentions from yourself or others, you can begin to create some incantations. Incantations begin changing your beliefs from the inner workings of your subconscious mind outward into your reality.

Your ego or personality is usually the point of connection in a relationship. Most relationships do not connect beyond this level. However, this is just a very small part of who we are. If you really desire to integrate your relationship with another person, if you desire the fabric to be woven together on a deeper personal level, you have to open up and connect your subconscious mind. The way this is accomplished is through incantations.

If you've got self-statements in your subconscious mind that are contrary to the desires you want in your life and the kind of relationship you desire, you have got to change that first. The way you change it is through incantations. These are positive commands that you say over and over and over again that eventually seep into your sub-conscious mind. You can say them together when you're working out, when you're making love, or alone when you're exercising, meditating, driving to work or any part of the day. The idea is to get these positive thoughts in your mind so your mind doesn't have room for fears and doubts anymore. Essentially, through the use of incantations and affirmations, you are changing your belief system.

When you believe something different, you attract something different. Incantations help your mind stay open to its highest potential and change your subconscious to begin attracting the kind of life, relationship and love you desire.

Creative Visualization can be a wonderful tool for rewiring your subconscious mind. Imagine the two of you in a magical circle together where nothing can penetrate it; no unwanted thoughts, no unwanted people and no unwanted ideas. Visualize the two of you together in this beautiful, magical circle filled with light, joy, love, passion and pleasure. Imagine it. It's yours.

Your objective is to create a magical circle that the relationship operates in. For example, if you believe that your partner has a wandering eye, consider sitting down together and creating a magical circle. There needs to be sacred understanding, no matter what the understanding is. These understandings will give you the power to create a magical circle. Once you have created this circle, start to empower it by visualizing the qualities you desire to have in yourself and the qualities you want to see in your mate. Next, visualize the qualities the two of you will have together as a team. So, what are some of the qualities that you desire to have in a relationship? Remember, write them down.

I believe the number one quality that must be within the sacred circle of a relationships is an undeniable, unstoppable trust. What is trust based on? It's based on people giving their word and keeping it. Trust is about making promises, giving your word, and then keeping it over and over and over again. Pretty soon, both parties begin to trust. They just know that they know.

The second part is about competence. Competence is about building the kind of skills that you need for the relationship with the person of your dreams. Everyone has different needs, wants and desires. No two people are alike, so you need someone who is competent enough to want to develop the skills and traits that you require in a relationship and vice versa. Trust gives a sense of freedom, so lovers don't have to be on guard all the time. When there is trust there is complete freedom to love freely.

Truth is a quality that goes hand in hand with trust. You can lie to yourself and you can lie to the world, but you CANNOT lie in the sacred circle of your relationship. You must lay down your sword when you walk into that sacred circle. There's no use for the sword in the circle.

As you work with the Law of Attraction to strengthen the circle of your relationship, it can't strengthen love if there is lying going on. **Lying is a counter-intention.** You need to be up front and truthful. A great bonding activity in a new relationship is to create a night where you share all the beliefs that you hold, experiences you've been through, actions you've taken and regrets you may have. Put it out on the table and create a circle of trust. This will make your circle stronger; giving it the ability to attract positive energies. By the way, if you've been married for 20 years, it's not too late to do this. There always has to be trust and truth in every relationship.

There is an interesting exercise that can help you get a clear picture and overall vision of your relationship as you strengthen your circle of trust and truth. This exercise is to "begin with the end in mind." This is a mediation where you visualize the last day of your life. This is based in part on an exercise from the book, <u>The Seven Habits of Highly Effective People</u> by Steven Covey.

Picture yourself lying on your deathbed. What are you saying to yourself as you lie in that bed? Will you say, "I wish I had made more money; I wish I had spent more time on the golf course; or, I wish I had spent more time in the office?" The answer is probably none of the above. What most people say is, "I wish I had spent more time nurturing the relationships that are important to me." So, what is it that you visualize as you are lying in your death bed? Do you see a life filled with love and close relationships? Do you see a life where you gave more than you took? Do you see a life of no regrets? If this is the legacy you desire to leave behind, what actions are you going to take *now* to make this vision a reality? That's beginning with the end in mind.

So, here is my question to you: do you really desire to start your life beginning with the end in mind, or do you desire to be like everybody else and jump into the pool of uncertainty hoping that you are going in the right direction? I think it makes more sense to begin with the end in mind; to look at the end of your life and say, "These are the values I find important: my relationships with my children, family, and dear friends." Protect relationships with people that are important to your life. You only have a little bit of time here, 60, 80, maybe 90 years, who knows? Focus your life on what's really important. **On your last day when you're about to take your last gasp of air, you're not going to wish you had spent more time at**

the office or golf course, but you will regret not spending more time with the people you love.

If you're in a relationship that's breaking up, take a good look to see what techniques mentioned here can help you. Once upon a time, you both had a seed of light and spirit which transferred from you to your love and back again. This seed is not gone, it was just neglected. You need to water and fertilize your love. Perhaps you'll desire to try to save your relationship, or use the experiences from a past relationship to empower you to have an even more extraordinary relationship in the future. Here's the secret! When a relationship ends, you think you'll never be able to replace that person. The truth is that you won't because everybody's unique, but it might be possible to find a replacement that's more compatible, more certain, more absolute than the lover or lovers of the past. My point is, if the relationship is over with, it's time to move on and create a better love.

It's important that there is a sense of love, truth and trust in the relationship. When this is happening, you are empowering that relationship to attract more of the same energy. **Whatever energies you throw into your circle of love is what the Universe will give you more of because likes attract likes.** This is a basic premise of all magic and the Law of Attraction: birds of a feather flock together. Create love attraction by filling your circle with love, caring, light, truth, and trust. What do I mean by light? I'm talking about illumination. Create a relationship where you are not biting your tongue all the time. Loving relationships have an environment where you are speaking openly and fluidly so the relationship keeps getting better. Most people think the best part of a relationship is the "honeymoon period" during the first year. You often hear older people say, "They'll settle in eventually." Older couples are saying that they will settle into a monotonous, boring relationship. It does not have to be this way though. Whatever you have in the first year can be twice as good in the second year, four times as good in the third year, and eight times as good in the fourth year. See what I'm saying? If you work together with love, caring, light, truth, trust and openness, you can actually continue to improve the quality of your relationship. It's up to you. **When you are making a conscious effort to enhance your love, you will see the Law of Attraction and the Universe are working with you.** You will begin to attract more of what you desire in your life. You are literally sending up signs to the Universe and saying, this is who I am. This is what I'm all about and I'm going to attract more of it.

When looking at creating the love of your life, you must also look at compassion. I have a friend who is very big in the business world. His wife was about 30 years younger than him and a knock-out model. In the morning she would call out, "Fraaank." Frank would look over his morning newspaper at her to find every pill he needed laid out on the table for him. This is because she had compassion and sense of caring for him. So, their relationship continued to prosper until the day he died. It prospered emotionally, mentally, spiritually and in every single way. Whatever level your relationship is at, if both of you are on the same page, you can reach a new level. **The Law of Attraction responds to what you are *vibrating* and brings you more of the same.** Your love gets even better! There will be exponential growth!

What about creative visualization to improve your relationship? At night before you fall asleep, create a visualization circle of love. Do this in your mind. What does the relationship look like when the two of you are together, happy and both on the same page? What does it look like when you're in the center of your circle? What does your love sound like? How do you talk to each other? How do you communicate? What kind of music do you listen to together? Are you badgering each other constantly or freely moving together in a new direction? Are the sounds of your relationship the sounds of two people in love and harmony? What about feeling? What does your visualization circle of love feel like? When you're in harmony, do you feel secure? You can visualize anything you desire your love to be in your mind. Napoleon Hill said, *"Whatever the mind of man can conceive and believe it can achieve."* **The keyword here is "believe"**; the mind must conceive an idea that it *believes* in. Creating belief begins by breaking down the sub-modalities of your creative visualization circle. What does it look like? What does it feel like? What does it taste like? Does your love life taste like candy or carrots? You get the idea. Engage all your senses in your visualization.

Reinforce the qualities you desire in your relationship. Reinforce looking good, sounding good, feeling good, and all of those qualities flowing in harmony. The more you begin to visualize love and see it, the more you begin to attract the entire power of the Universe to aid in your creating perfect love. The Universe will begin vibrating around your circle, bringing you what you desire. **I personally believe that you can create an incredible circle of love that only you and your lover can ever enter; it can never be**

breached. Yes, circles can be broken and shattered, but if the two of you are living within that circle and keeping it strong, it can last forever.

We're living in a fast food society where most relationships are only lasting a year and a half. We're throwing away our relationships as fast as we throw away our fast food containers. This is the world we live in and its not likely to change anytime soon. However, you can change yourself, your life, your potential and you can have everything you desire in life through the Law of Attraction.

One way of making permanent inner changes is through incantations. Incantations are types of affirmations that are designed to talk to your subconscious mind and transform it. The challenge with the subconscious mind is that, while your conscious mind has goals, beliefs and directions, your subconscious mind may be filled with counter-intentions or the opposite goals and beliefs. In other words, you could be sabotaging yourself without even knowing it. For those of you who have been in a series of unsuccessful relationships, you may aware that there is some kind of self-sabotage going on there. You can change that. Miracle Mentoring and Alchemy Life Coaching can expose your counter-intentions and give you the tools to write customized incantations that will change the context in your subconscious mind. You have the power to make your subconscious mind work to create love. It's very important that the subconscious mind is working with you because, if it's not working for you, it's working against you. There's no neutrality in the subconscious mind; it's either empowering you or holding you back. Remember that incantations are different than affirmations in that they provide a direct command to the subconscious mind. Here is an example of an incantation, *"I command my subconscious mind to awaken every part of my brain and my nervous system to the energy and vibration of love. My lover and I are drawing closer to each other, moment by moment. Every part of my body and mind are in harmony with loving, joyful, happy and empowering relationship."*

Let's talk about actions you can take when a relationship is about to break up. Don't text or call you lover every five minutes. Stop sending music that you've recorded. Stop sending emails around the clock. Nobody wants to be harassed. If you've broken up recently, harassing events can send the relationship to an even deeper negative spiral. Give the person space. Do the inner plane work and circle visualization. This work is about expecting the kind of relationship you desire. Don't blow up on the phone. Rather, begin working on yourself.

This is a time to carefully explore the reasons for the relationship. Are you looking to mutually help fulfill each other's deepest desires along with your goals as a couple? Are you just afraid of being alone? Do you belief that there is no one else that can love you in a deeper, more satisfying way? How can you expect the Law of Attraction to help you with your relationship when you're not even strengthening your own energy field? Most people don't care where you're at now; they want to know and see who you're going be in the future.

Here is an incantation example to use, **"I command my unconscious mind to transform me into a calm, confident, relaxed**

and strong individual." After a break up, you need to operate from a position of personal power. The idea is to become magnetic again to your mate and to all the other people around you. So saying this incantation thousand times a day will seriously empower you. It's a good incantation for creating the energy that first attracted your mate.

You are the defender of your sacred circle. Your relationship is a sacred circle. You need to start seeing it that way. If you don't treat it as if it's sacred, nobody else will either. Make it sacred from this moment on. You are the defender of your sacred circle of love. Remember, **what you see, feel and believe you will attract**.

CHAPTER 10: SOUL MATE SECRETS

"Try to be a rainbow

in someone's cloud."

Maya Angelou

Everyone wants to attract his or her soul mate, but what is a soul mate? There is much misconception about what a soul mate is. Just about everyone you talk to will give you a different definition. I am going to explain to you what a soul mate is based on my understanding from years of ancient mystery studies.

First, when you meet somebody and you fall "head over heels in love" or you have an immediate attraction to them, this is usually not your soul mate. Your soul mate, according to Kabbalistic tradition, is somebody that was created not physically, but spiritually at the same time that you were created. In other words, your souls were created together by the Lord of the Universe. You are part of the same creative "exhalation" or the same exhale of the spirit. Often, people mistake animal attractiveness and physical desire as a soul mate love. Even if you say after the first date, "We got along perfectly, we talked all night, and he/she was so attractive!" that's not necessarily your soul mate. Your soul mate is here not only to love you and share life with, but your soul mate is here to teach you and guide you as a partner, unlocking your highest potential as a couple.

That is very different than how Hollywood has portrayed the soul mate. Your soul mate is somebody that you can constantly grow deeper in love with; the more time you spend together the more you feel, and the more you feel, the more time you desire to spend together. As you grow in knowledge and emotional connection, the fires of love and life continue to grow. You live life together as one unit. You want to share your ideals. It doesn't mean you have the same ideals, but your ideals start to merge. Your relationship develops a unique synergy. No longer is it about your ideals as a man or her ideals as a woman, it melts into a third type of ideal. There's a third creation that takes place and it is almost like giving birth

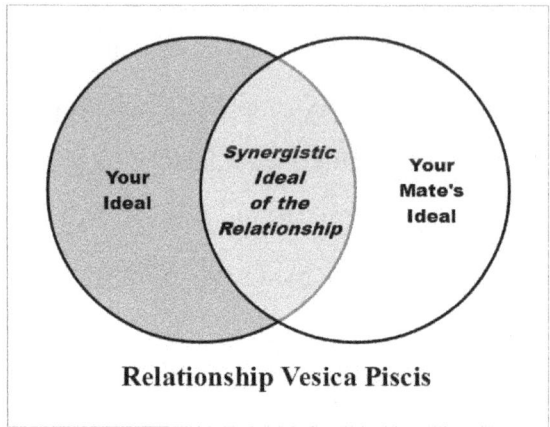

Relationship Vesica Piscis

to a child. The child represents the soul mate connection between two individuals. The mystics depicted this artistically, often as the "Christ child" or a spiritual figure in the center of a vesica piscis. The vesica piscis is a symbol of union between two people who open themselves up to receive a higher state of consciousness. Whether they are aware of it or not, that illustrates their connection of finding each other.

How do we test for a soul mate? I'm not sure that there is a 100% test. However, muscle testing will often reveal a great deal along with the use of spiritual hypnosis. Can you have multiple soul mates? Some people say that you can and while others say there's only one. Whichever belief you hold, the universe will support. I do know that in the process of connecting with your soul mate, every part of your life becomes integrated on a mental, physical, spiritual and financial level.

I have a client who has not integrated with his wife. They have separate finances and properties; everything is separated. In other words, there's no merging of funds or energies. They even take separate vacations at times. It makes me wonder why they are even together. Maybe they are just together to co-create the species by having children. Over a period of time, they have not followed the soul mate tendency to merge all the different aspects of their lives together to make a third creation.

A couple that are truly soul mates, create a relationship that manifest into an exchange that is not "you," and is not "I," but becomes "us." It's not your way or my way, it's *our* way. Let me make this truth clear, it's not about compromising. This is very important. Soul mates don't compromise. Soul mates, when they are with each other, are almost uncompromising. True soul mates find this unique place that doesn't require compromise. It is a place where, all of a sudden, new opportunities begins to click and manifest. It is a third way that is born. Soul mates find this place and attach themselves to it. When they "throw themselves on the fire," they create a whole new energy. A creation wheel begins to turn in a positive way through the combined effort of the soul mates.

That being said, I don't think life is always easy for soul mates in the beginning. Sometimes, I think they give up too soon. I mentored a couple many years ago that I was absolutely certain were soul mates. I spendt many hours mentoring them as a couple but at some point they went their separate directions. Over the years I have kept in contact with them and I can tell you beyond any shadow of a doubt that they have never been as complete, happy and totally absorbed in life and love as when they were together.

I saw in this couple that they often contained the same qualities. I could see that they were created from the same cloth. Often, they had so much in common and their lives were paralleled in so many familiar ways that the familiarity was almost too much to bear. In the beginning of a true soul mate journey it almost feels better to find a mate out there who is different. The truth of the matter is that you won't find a different mate who will be better.

Your soul mate will challenge you and believe in you. When the rest of the world tells you "No!", your soul mate says, "I believe in you and there's nothing stopping you." Your soul mate knows the spirit that lives within your soul because he or she shares it as well. A soul mate will believe in you because they always desire the best for you. When you are with you soul mate, you will find that there's a part of them that is almost self-sacrificing to the point that they would throw themselves on the railroad tracks so you can move forward in life. They are willing to sacrifice themselves because they love the other person that much.

There are all kinds of incredible qualities to soul mates. Sometimes you see soul mates that say, "We've been fighting too much. What are we going to do?" Let me ask you, what are you fighting about? Is it because you're both stubborn in ideas, beliefs and concepts? Is it because you are both off the same tree? Perhaps it's because you are truly soul mates that you are fighting. There are methods through creative visualization to change stubborn aspects of the relationship. Sometimes growing with your soul mate doesn't come easy; creating the third way is not an easy experience to manifest.

Your soul mate may not be love at first sight. Let me illustrate this with a story about "Uncle Mac." (Mac was not a true relative but was given "Uncle" as an honorary title.) Uncle Mac was a high school teacher and his wife was a grade school teacher. He was spiritual man. He and his wife came to live with me for about two weeks; which was there custom. These people were in their 80's when they were living with me. They often lived with different people for about two weeks at a stretch as Uncle Mac mentored and shared his spirituality with his hosts.

I can remember Uncle Mac and his wife leaving the house after dinner one night. They took a walk down the block, holding hands and talking. When they went out to dinner, they still talked as if they were on their first date; talking about their hopes and dreams for the future.

At one point, his wife was in the hospital. The doctors said she wouldn't make it through the night. She had a massive heart attack and they didn't give her but a few hours. So, he knelt down next to her bed and prayed for her all night. The next morning she opened her eyes and said, "Mac, I'm really hungry for some ice cream." They hugged and cried and he knew she was going to be okay. These two people were soul mates. They spent more than 50 years together in love. However, it wasn't about the time they spent together; it was the fact that, in the beginning, their relationship wasn't perfect. Step-by-step he sacrificed his male ego to make it perfect for her. She sacrificed all the hen pecking and advice from mothers and girlfriends who wanted to influence her relationship in order to be a perfect wife for him. They became perfect for each other and they never stopped romancing, they never stopped loving. That's the way they ended their lives, in love.

Uncle Mac and his wife were more mentors to me than anyone else in my life. He was an incredible mentor. I only spent a short time with them but the love and passion he had for his wife and she had for him was never lacking in their relationship.

So how do you want to feel with you soul mate? Uncle Mac knew how he wanted to feel in his relationship and he took action to create it. The first step is to know how you desire to feel. Do you desire a soul mate in your life? Do you desire your marriage partner back in your life? Do you desire your lover back? Do you desire a life full of love, passion and joy? Then, know how you desire to feel. If you don't know or think about it or write it down, then you can't attract it. It's not about money, it's not about where you live and it's not about your job. It's about HOW YOU WANT TO FEEL. How do you desire to feel with the person you love? How do the two of you want to feel together?

There is no power on this Earth greater than two people in love who share a dream. People who dream together, share their hopes and discuss their greatest desires together tend to stay together.

This is because, in that process, you are giving the most intimate part of yourself. Are you willing to give the most intimate part of yourself? How do you want to feel in your relationship? It's not about what you want to do in your relationship; it's about how you desire to feel. Do you desire to feel cared for, safe, nurtured and loved?

The Law of Attraction facilitates in creating the feelings you desire in your relationship. What are you creating in your mind? Thinking about it will cause you to attract the relationship you desire. **Make your soul mate connection the dominating thought in your mind. This is the secret to attracting the love your desire.**

I love the story that Steven Covey shared about a man coming up to him after a workshop. The man says that he has a problem because he doesn't feel any love for his wife any more. Steven Covey then responds, "Love her." The man tries to explain and says, "You don't understand, I don't feel anything for her, there's no spark there." Steven responds back, "Then love her." (The 7 Habits of Highly Effective People by Steven Covey - Published by Simon & Schuster.)

Love is a verb. Being a soul mate is an action job. When you are in a relationship or you have a partnership, then you have to take some action. Love is that verb; love is that action; love is that energy. It is not stagnant. It's not just an emotion you feel, it's an action you TAKE. Love is who you ARE. It's a quality you LIVE. Are you willing to make that kind of commitment? Once you make that commitment you start attracting that kind of good energy around you and what you're putting out starts coming back to you. It may not be immediate or overnight. Don't call me a week from now and say,

"Well, I tried." **You don't try, you do.** You are either a lover of spirit and a lover of the soul, or you're not.

When attracting your soul mate, it is absolutely important to become a fitting container. This is a powerful teaching of some of the early mystics. They realized that if you desired something, you had to be a container to hold it. You wouldn't put acid in a plastic container. It's not a fitting container for acid because the acid would eat right through it and end up all over the place. You wouldn't put water in a straw basket because the basket wouldn't hold the water.

So, what is a fitting container for love? It's simple. Sit down with the one you love and ask: What is it that makes you feel loved? What is it that makes you feel safe? What is it that makes you feel good? What gives you hope? What helps you visualize almost impossible dreams we can create together?

If you don't have somebody and you're looking to attract someone in your life, perhaps you need to lose a few pounds, shave, take care of yourself and look the best you can. You need to become a fitting container for the type of person you desire to attract. Maybe you desire to take an English class and stop using foul language or stop smoking.

I mentored a man once who smoked cigarettes and smelled to high heaven of tobacco. He had all kinds of opportunities going for him but could not get the type of girl he wanted. He said he only attracted women who drank, smoked and used foul language. I asked where he met these women and he told me he met them at the local bar. So, I looked at him with his three-day-beard, his smell of smoke and his foul language and said, "I think you may be attracting these women on purpose. What would happen if you met a woman with an education? Would you be comfortable?" He told me he thought women like that were stuck up. He had preconceived notions about different types of women. Women play the same games with men; it works both ways. This man was not a fitting container to attract a nice career girl. He certainly was not a fitting container for attracting his soul mate. He had the wrong beliefs and was looking in the wrong places.

You have to decide what qualities you desire in a soul mate. Don't be so shallow as to only engage in small talk; when you meet someone special talk about life long dreams. Talk about deep emotional qualities that you would like to see in your soul mate. Adjust your thoughts and habits to become a fitting container for those qualities.

Developing some power incantations is one way to help you become a fitting container. What do you believe about yourself? What is your potential? What do you feel about yourself at a core level? If you have limiting beliefs, like so many of us do, you need to change those with some powerful incantations and affirmations.

There are some very specific secrets on how to create these incantations. There's a right way and wrong way. The right way is to take your fears and invert them. Write incantations that are based on the opposite of your fears. These incantations are self-talk that become part of your subconscious thinking process. Avoid using words like "don't" and "won't" because the subconscious mind cancels these words out. With a change in your subconscious, you'll start attracting the kind of people you desire to attract and have the relationship you deserve. Until you change your inner beliefs, you'll never move forward into a soul mate relationship. Here is an example of an incantation to attract your soul mate, *"I command my subconscious mind to muster all the elements of my brain, nervous system, entire body, and energy field to attracting my soul mate into my life for a loving, lifelong fulfilling relationship. I am filled with confidence and absolute certainty that my soul mate is entering my reality."*

You deserve to have incredible love. You deserve the relationship you really desire. The Magic of Light, the Power of Spirit and the power of the Law of Attraction are all tools that you can put to work for you. Banish all fears that hold you back from attracting your soul mate.

CHAPTER 11: LOVE AND THE LAW OF ATTRACTION

"As to me I know of

nothing else but miracles."

Walt Whitman

I am convinced that you can have extraordinary accomplishments in your life if you put time and effort into learning the richness and depth of the ancient mysteries. Some people are born just knowing these secrets. Perhaps, it's a past life carry-over, the way they were raised, or maybe it is just a mystery of the Universe. I have a friend who is as intelligent as you will find anywhere in the world, has a nice personality, is fairly well educated, and has accomplished great wonders in the past. However, what he's doing now is just unbelievable. He's living in the back of his van!

What does that tell you? It tells you that there's a secret he's forgotten. He isn't happy living in the back of his van; he wants more out of life. In fact, we all desire more. No matter where you're at in life or what your status is, it is normal to desire more. My friend could have the life he desires, the home he wants, and the love he craves. However, because of his situation, he eats really crappy food and that makes him unhealthy, which makes his energy field unattractive creating a downward spiral that works against him.

Some of you are in a negative energy cycle right now. You

make statements like, "No matter what I do, I can't lose five pounds and every time I lose five pounds I gain ten back," or "No matter how many times I try, I can't quit smoking," or "No matter how many hours a day I work, I can't seem to get ahead and make the money I desire to meet my needs." Every human being has the potential to be incredibly happy. You could be full of joy, shining light, glowing with happiness, experiencing abundance and living the "good life", but you lack the knowledge of the ancient secrets. If my friend living in the van would take the time to learn the ancient secrets, he could accomplish extraordinary wonders beyond his wildest dreams.

When I refer to the "ancient secrets" I am referring to the secrets that were taught in the mystery schools of ancient Egypt, Greece, early Christianity and the Kabbalistic schools. One of the modern mystery schools that still teaches these secrets is "The Esoteric Order of the Golden Dawn". (I am the Imperator General of this ancient order for men and women. Learn more about the ancient knowledge at www.esotericgoldendawn.com.) There are a few people who know these secrets instinctively, but most people have to learn them. What stops most people from learning the ancient mysteries is that it take years and years of study. I have been teaching these ancient mysteries for 30 plus years and have been a student of the Ancient Mysteries of Light for many more years. This is the knowledge that shifts your energy field to bring miracles into your life through employing the Law of Attraction.

I regularly see this energy shift in my Miracle Mentoring and Alchemy Life Coaching with my clients. As I teach them the ancient secrets, everything in their lives starts to change. The end result is that they now live making an above average income. Some of my clients have even gone from being broke to great wealth.

So, where did the ancient mystery of the Law of Attraction come from? It came from the wise old sage, Hermes Trismegistus. He was an ancient Egyptian sage, who some believe was a god, while others believe was an individual that had experienced enlightenment. Archaeologist have not discovered a biography for Hermes Trismegistus yet, so defining his life is wrapped in mystery. Archaeologist have discovered that those sacred words, **"As above, so below"** are first seen written in "The Emerald Tablets of Hermes".

The key to life lies in those ancient words, "As above, so below". The reason you are not attracting into life all your desires is because in the above, which is your mind, you're focused on negativity, fears and anxieties. No matter how hard you try, without the ancient knowledge to eradicate those fears or without the mystery secrets revealing the power to eliminate anxiety, you keep making the same mistakes over and over again. **Without new knowledge creating new ways to approach life, you keep getting the same results.**

Everyone desires more money and love. I know of several of Law of Attraction gurus who make their focus on attracting money. I think it is absurd how much some of them just focus only on money. Money is great! There's nothing wrong with money. If you desire more money, you should have more money. If you're making $100,000, you can be making $200,000; if that's what you desire. However, I believe that the real nectar of life, the real juice of life is *love*.

Love is the healer. Love excites the entire matrix of the Universe giving your energy field life and vitality. Every marriage starts with this passion permeating every waking moment of the relationship. The majority of my Miracle Mentoring and Alchemy Life Coaching clients are women. In the one-on-one mentoring I do with them, many of them say, "Robert, I'm in a loveless marriage and I'm tired of it. I've been married for 15 years and this guy comes home, flicks on the TV and expects dinner, then he goes out with his buddies. Occasionally we have a date night followed by mediocre sex. I am not really sure why I stick around in the marriage." So, where is the Universal love in most marriages? Marriages tend to become boring; those who were once lovers are now tired. Somewhere along the line, love is replaced with marriage and simply "playing house".

Then there are these wonderful human beings who are just exotic in the way they go about life. They are peacocks, fanning their tails and strutting their stuff. They have the fastest car, castle like homes, swimming pools, club memberships, executive jobs, everything you could possibly imagine; they have it all. Sadly, many of these people are driving down the long highway of life alone.

When I mentor these types they say, "Robert, I have no idea. I have more money than most of the people I know. I work harder than those around me. I have more things, I go more places, and I have more to offer but others around me who have so much less to give seem to have everything going for them. They seem to have all the love they need and I don't. What can I do about it?" I ask these people whether they desire a loving relationship or are they just looking to add love to the list of their possessions. Are you seeking

105

love just to "keep up with the Joneses"?

I mentored a gentleman about three years ago who created great wealth in the stock market. He had a fast car, a wonderful place to live, but didn't have anyone to love. When he finally got into a relationship, he was miserable. He approached a relationship the way he might purchase a new car. Who wants that kind of love?

There are those couples who once felt love but are now just playing house in a legal contract called *"marriage"*. There are those that have everything and just want to add love to their list of possessions. Then, there is the relationship where one individual is constantly in this state of asking, "What about me?" This is a type of selfish love that puts the other partner into slavery. If both partners are saying this, it is double the trouble.

The couple that finds themselves in the "what about me relationship" will be in constant pain. In this kind of relationship, there are two people that both, for some reason, have pain where they once had love. Maybe one person's pain is more legitimate than another's, but pain is pain. Couples who have been arguing for years and years about who is suffering the most have lost sight of love. True love can talk about pain and find a way to transform the pain into pleasure.

I don't know what kind of relationship you have. I hope you are blessed with a wonderful, loving, caring, nurturing, light-filled relationship with happiness, joy, sexual pleasure and everything you need. If you don't have the love you crave, utilizing the Law of Attraction will transform your love life. The Law of Attraction affects all situations in your life; it's not just about making money, you can use it for love as well. You are probably using the Law of Attraction already in your relationships but you may be using it in a negative way.

Let me give you an example of using the Law of Attraction in a negative way. You get up in the morning, you look at yourself in the mirror and see a quality you do not like. You see that you're a little skinny, or a little overweight, or your hips are wide, or there's a new wrinkle on your face. Now, you immediately start to think negatively about yourself. What a "great" way to start the day. During your day you see a beautiful woman or a handsome guy. The problem is that now you're afraid to start up a conversation or start a relationship because the first activity of your morning was rejecting yourself. There is now an expectation that everyone else will reject you, too. You have a negative Law of Attraction script playing in your head.

We are all here. We all came into this world the same way and we're all going out the same way. Nobody is better than you. You are unique, you are special and you need to focus on what makes you unique and special. Focus on those parts of your personality that make you stand out, feel good about yourself, and begin to love yourself.

One of the exercises that my Qigong instructor friend does is a wonderful way to start loving and accepting yourself. During the Qigong class, he instructs the repetition of different mantras while touching various parts of the body. He will have you say, "This is my kidney, I love my kidney. These are my lungs. I love my lungs. This is my liver. I love my liver. This is my heart, I love my heart." He continues instructing this way until you have touched and loved your whole body. It's a simplistic exercise and when you think about it, it's almost child-like.

The truth of the matter is that you need to love yourself. This is the first step. If you don't love yourself and feel absolutely confident that you can be he answer to another person's dream, you'll hesitate and you'll show lack of confidence. You'll express disempowerment and that is what you will attract in your love. You will attract the opposite of your dream mate with your lack of confidence and fear.

How about if you are a single parent who is always thinking, "Who is going to want to be with me? I have three children that I am raising on my own!"? This is a negative Law of Attraction belief. Focus on being the best single parent you can be. Change your thoughts by saying, "I will attract the love of my life who is waiting to adopt my wonderful children." Change your limiting beliefs and start loving. Yes, you CAN attract the kind of person you desire.

Perhaps, the people you keep attracting lack excitement; they lack that juice and charisma that you seek. Odds are, it is because you are afraid and you have low self-esteem. Many of you are staying in a horrible relationship because you believe you'll never attract a better relationship. All these limiting beliefs are killing your love life. You're attracting a lack of love by your negative affirmations and your negative self-perception. Once you begin to change your own inner landscape, look in the mirror and love yourself. Other people will find it much easier to love you, too.

We all have been told that "love hurts", but it does not have to hurt all the time. You can choose to change how you love yourself and change how others love you. Imagine that there are two doors of love. Behind door number one, there is someone crying and complaining about life. Behind door number two, there is someone standing there with refreshments, slippers, soft music and candle light. Which door do you think you are going to walk through? Of course, you are going to walk through the door where pleasure, happiness, and joy are being expressed.

So many people today have been through such traumatic, horrible, nasty relationships that all they can express is pain. Every time somebody touches their hand, they want to cry because they are anchored to that past pain. Unless you change and break those anchors, every time you see someone that might be a person worth getting to know better, you're still going to awaken that old pain. You are standing behind door number one, which is the door few people desire to walk through. Holding on to your pain and fear is going to turn off possible lovers. People desire to walk through the door where there is happiness and joy taking place. If you cannot create this, there is work to do on yourself. Working on yourself will help you start attracting the people you desire into your life. A great way to start changing yourself from the inside out is to clear your chakras. The "Chakra Cleaning & Mindbody Healing Program" is available at www.lawofattractionsolutions.com

It works in reverse, too. I often run into guys who say, "I really like this girl. I met her not too long ago. We met over coffee and went to dinner the next day. She told me her problems with her ex-husband and her ex before that. She shared all the trouble she got into and the pain she went through. I feel so bad for her. I spent four hours listening to her ..." and so on. WOW, this new relationship is being founded in past pain.

Usually men, but sometimes women, think in their mind that somehow listening to someone else's problems is going to endear them and make them a special lover. Think about this: do you really desire the first experience you have with someone to be a "pain party"? Do you want to share "date" experiences where others tell you all of their problems, heartache, pain, anxiety, and a ton of low-energy vibration experiences? What usually happens is someone tells you all this stuff, then later you become a part of their "pain party", not their lover. They identify you with the pain, heartache, etc. You think you are being loving by listening to them talk to you for four hours about their pain, but when the date is over, there are no memories of happiness.

On the other hand, if you go out dancing with someone else who does not trap you in their pain party, you have just associated joy, happiness and fun with that person. The whole idea when beginning a new relationship is to associate pleasure with the relationship. This means not inviting someone to your pain party or allowing yourself to be dragged into their pain party.

Pain parties create negative emotional anchors to you, even though you have now become their best friend. I call it the "Uncle syndrome", in which you will get introduced to the phrase, "Hey, this is my best friend!" You have become the best friend, not the lover. This is because best friends are the people that listen to all the problems. So, the next time you feel inclined to listen to a potential lover's problems, the less likely you are to develop a relationship with that person. Note: This is not true once a relationship is well established and people are getting to know each other on a deeper level.

Consider this: when somebody starts a conversation by talking about their biker ex who did this and that, you should start to listen then you immediately do what is called "break state." Get the person's mind out of his or her own pain and into the present moment. Maybe you pick up a coffee cup and drop it. That's a little dramatic but it will break the state. Perhaps you grab your chest, clutch it and fall to the ground. Now, that's REALLY dramatic, but it will definitely break the state. There are easier ways to do it, too. You might say something such as, "You mentioned your ex is a biker, do you like to go fast? Have you ever been on a speedboat before? I would love to take you out on a speedboat sometime. We could travel up and down the river at 120mph."

Now, you've got excitement, exhilaration and positive energy, but more importantly, you've broken the negative state. You've taken her or him out of their negative state and moved them to a positive one. This makes more sense than participating in someone's "pain party". The technique of breaking state is a great way to insure you stay on the path to becoming a lover.

Another secret to enhancing love is using the neurolinguistics techniques called anchoring. It's a very simple technique that is easy to use. The next time you're dating someone you really like, look for the SIGNS OF HAPPINESS. A sign of happiness is anything that a person does when they're expressing something that really makes them happy or turns them on; something that really excites them. Learn the movements they make in a state of happiness. It could be the way they use their eyes, purse their lips, make gestures, or any number of movements. Now, as you watch and observe, being careful not to reveal what you are doing, you will now invoke a technique called MIRRORING. It's very simple. If they put their palms up, as if they are receiving something when they talk about happy memories, when you desire them to feel happy, create that anchor and turn your palms up. As you do it again and again, you will awaken those happy feeling and they will be anchored to you.

Isn't that key to what love is really about? It is about helping each other to feel safe and feel good. It isn't about just getting along in life. I know from experience that this is true. Relationships are about making the other person feel special, feel good, feel wonderful, feel happy; that's what love is about. It's about making the person feel safe, secure, cared for and joyful. This is very, very important. I'm going to be REALLY honest with you now. You don't have unlimited time; I don't care if you're ten years old. In truth, no matter how many wonderful experiences you have as you move through other peoples' lives, the chances of creating true love require your full mental and emotional attention. So when you do meet a special someone, cherish them with all your heart. It's about making yourself feel good on the inside and sharing it with the world on the outside. As you share your positive feelings, emotions, and optimistic expectations, the Law of Attraction will bring you opportunities for love. What you do with these opportunities is up to you.

CHAPTER 12: ENERGY HEALING AND THE LAW OF ATTRACTION

"I have decided to be happy

because it's good for my health."

Voltaire

I would like to spend this chapter addressing the interesting subject of energy healing as it works in relationship with the Law of Attraction. How many of you have been to an energy healer? How many have sat down with a mystic and had them lay their hands upon you while you were creating an intention for wellness? One of the problems is there are some exceptionally good energy healers out there, but there are many that simply do not understand the Law of Attraction. If you are looking for an energy healer, you need to test their knowledge on the Law of Attraction first.

All energy healing is directly responsive to the Law of Attraction. There is no other basis. That which is created above must manifest below and that which is created below will be reflected in the world above. This was the teaching of the ancient Egyptians and of Hermes in the writing referred to as "The Emerald Tablet." In the ancient world, the secrets of the Emerald Tablet were considered so valuable that people died protecting them. The secrets in Hermes' Tablet also led to schools springing up all over the world, such as the

Kabbalist Schools and the Christian Mystery Schools. While the outer teachings are different, the core teachings are the same. The Emerald Tablet is filled with knowledge that will shift the way you interact with the world.

Some metaphysical scholars who have studied the Emerald Tablet say that it contains "pre-shift" knowledge. They see it as the knowledge that helped create the event some people call "The 2012 Shift". It doesn't matter if you believe in massive shifts or not, the truth of the matter is that there is a shift going on in the world. Human consciousness is elevating in awareness of how every action affects life as we understand it.

One of the results of shifting consciousness is that there are energy healers popping up on every corner. The problem is that they have not studied or don't fully understand the nature of the Emerald Tablet and the Law of Attraction. I believe this knowledge becomes very important as a vital tool in all energy healing. If you understand how it works, you can make it work better. If you don't understand the concept of Hermetics and the teachings of the Law of Attraction, you are missing a few tools from your tool box.

It doesn't matter how many initiations or attunements you've had to become an energy healer. What really matters is if you are in alignment with the Universe and if you are connecting with Universal Energy on a level that is higher than the illness. If you can do that, you can truly become an exceptional energy healer and facilitate miracles in peoples' lives. For Christians, the highest source of universal healing light is Jesus. In other religious belief systems, healing light is called by different names.

There's nothing more shocking than to have a doctor say, "Look, you're not going to walk again.". However, with the help of an energy healer, you begin to walk. This kind of incredible miracle is not caused by the of the techniques of the healer, but caused by their deep understanding of the Law of Attraction and an intimate connection with Divine Source, Light, Jesus or God. Powerful healers understand the concept of setting up an important intention for the Law of Attraction to amplify. Your belief about the situations is the prerequisite for the outcome of healing work. **If you don't believe it can happen, if you are coming up with excuses, then forget it. It is not going to happen.**

Most energy healers find that people seek them out when traditional medical science, nutritionist, chiropractors and everyone else in town, have been given up on them . Most people don't seem to come to energy healers to make them feel better or assist in a smooth passing over to the other side. Most of them come because the energy healer is the last door on the block. They knock on that door out of desperation and they hope the energy healer can help them accomplish a miracle no one else could. The majority of the population has not been clearly exposed to energy healing so they come seeking restored health for their body with the attitude that they are wishing on a star.

The only way that an energy healer has the ability to be that wish on a shooting star is if the healer can connect to the Universal Law of Attraction. If a healer cannot create the clients vitality, health, energy and healing in the higher planes of consciousness, then no matter what method, symbol, or prayers are used, the patient is still going to stay sick, get sicker or even die. We all know everyone is going to die at some point. I agree with most healers that we can't always use death as the absolute sign of success or failure of energy healing. The truth is that not all energy healing can be measured by current science and you don't know what other influences the client might have on their health.

Let me give you an example of energy healing that worked but death still followed. On several occasions, I have had the privilege of being called to perform healing on terminally ill cancer patients who are in terrible pain. On one of these occasions, a young women who had bone cancer that had also spread to other vital organs called me in after everyone else had given up. The cancer had spread so much that even the gentle energy I projected out of my hands was too much pain for her body. I could not lay my hands on her body in the fashion I usually did because of the position that she had to place herself on the bed. This was a very severe case and I would like to note for those of you who believe you project out of the right hand and receive into your left, this was not an option. I had to get into positions where I projected out of my left and caught energy out of my right. It was most important in this case to allow my client to remain in a position that was most comfortable for her.

Despite the condition in which healing was done, we were making some interesting progress. Doctors verified that the spreading of the cancer was slowing down and my client's health seemed to be improving. The next time I went to give energy healing to the young lady, her health had suddenly taken a nose dive. I couldn't understand why her body had taken such a critical dive when we had just started to make progress. I found out later that somebody had come in and spoke to her about preparing for her death. Up until then, she was preparing to live by eradicating this cancer and pain. We were making progress! We weren't winning awards, but the cancer was slowing down. Once that idea was placed in her mind, "You need to make plans to die now. What kind of a funeral do you desire?" Her mind was creating her departure. I was very upset. Who cares what kind of funeral she wanted? The healing we were doing showed positive signs. We still had work to do! However, as the Emerald Tablet teaches, "as above, so below." The young lady's beliefs, which had been influenced by others, created her reality. It was not any lack on my part as an energy healer. Her mind had been made up. This shows how powerful the client's use of the Law of Attraction is in the healing process.

Unfortunately, shortly after that visit with the big discussion about preparing for the worst, my client began to slide downhill extraordinarily fast. I was still committed to helping her, so we then shifted the focus of our work. Our focus changed to reducing her pain. Sometimes, as an energy healer, you must change the protocol or goal of your work based on how your client responds.

In contrast to the beautiful young woman who died from her bone cancer, I had another lady in her 40's who had stage-4 cancer. She had lost her breasts, but there was still cancer in her lymph glands. Doctors wanted to put her on radiation and she said, "Look, it's just me and my 10 year old son. There is no way I can afford to lay down and start dying at the hands of chemotherapy!" She was brought to me in desperate circumstances, but she had an iron will. There was nothing in her mind that would counteract the healing she sought. She had the Law of Attraction working for her on an extraordinary level. I worked with her for 9 or 10 weeks. There were some tests done and there were no more markers of cancer in her body. Doctors tested again 3 months later and there was still no cancer. The point is that she got better, not because somebody knew the right Reiki symbol, word to vibrate, or planetary symbol. She got better because she created it in the higher planes of reality so that healing had to manifest in the lower planes. There was no choice.

In one case, a person wanted to live but everyone was telling her that she was going to die. In the other case, the person did not entertain all the negativity that the doctors said. There have been studies done where people were told, "You have a very good chance of surviving this cancer." Guess what? These people often do survive cancer. The studies also showed that when you tell patients they will be dead in a few weeks, they tend to die rather quickly. "As above, so below" is the lesson we must all heed.

The Emerald Tablet teaches how the Law of Attraction detects what you're thinking and then the Universe works to manifest those thoughts. You can't hide from this. If you know anybody who needs healing and they have counter-intentions in their subconscious, then the healing will be hindered or not work at all. If you don't have anyone who's trained and skilled at detecting the counter-intentions and reverse them, all healing efforts will be in vain. It is important for all energy healers to do the clearing work at each level of the healing process. The whole concept of energy healing revolves around the concept that if you can create it in a higher plane, it must manifest in the lower plane.

As an energy healer, I understand the Law of Attraction, but I also have other skills that assist me my energy healing work. My skills as a hypnotherapist and neurolinguistic specialist allow me to use language that will begin to shift a person's belief system. Hypnosis can help to reduce pain and open a person's subconscious mind to begin looking at their beliefs. I can help a client really dig into the depths of the subconscious mind to see some of the beliefs that are present, either working for or against our healing efforts. Hypnosis and Neurolinguistic Alchemy (a Spiritual form of NLP) allows an uncovering of what is in the client that is helping the healing efforts. It will also allow for an alchemical changing of anything hindering the healing efforts.

This is how I see holistic spiritual healing: our job is to shrink morbidity. We're all going to die. It's part of the alchemical process of change. Maybe we're going to change how it happens, when it happens or how long until it happens, but it's going to happen. The idea is that we desire to see people live long, happy, vibrant lives. We want to see people at 80 or 90 years old having a great time with a healthy body. We want to see you having a vibrant, fulfilling, wholesome life at whatever age you are. Then, when it is time, death will come quickly with very little or no sickness. In the case of my grandmother, she lived a vibrant life until, one day, she sat down at dinner, closed her eyes and fell asleep. This is what is called "compressed morbidity". **What we're working to eliminate is continuous mental and physical pain. No one needs to live like**

that.

All effective energy healers must be able to change the flow of energy. This can be done by energy clearing, playing singing bowls, working with crystal grids, Ruach Healing, Reiki, Angelic Healing Touch, meditation, and of course prayer. I love them all, but whatever is used, it must penetrate deeply to change the flow of energy.

I once worked with a client who almost died of a heart attack at age 25. Luckily, medics where able to revive him before he died. As I started exploring his energy during his first healing session, the thought came to mind, "What if he wants to die? What if he subconsciously, on a deep, emotional level, he is dying of a broken heart?" I began working on cleaning his lower chakras to establish a firm base. I used some basic hypnosis and Neurolinguistic Alchemy to help him enter a deeper meditative state. In the protection of my healing room in this deep relaxed state, this man was able to let out the pain of the vivid memories of tragically losing his mother at 3 years of age. It was quite a discovery, as a healer, to understand that this man's heart attack occurred because he had never released the loss of his mother. He didn't understand why this had happened to his mother. He was always in pain. This man was dying of a broken heart. His heart attack was not a tragedy that just randomly happened one day. It happened because his heart had been broken back at 3 years of age when he saw how painfully his mother died. As an energy healer, I had to first alchemically transform his pain, in order to begin changing his base for reality. As the Emerald Tablet states, "as above, so below." By helping him mend his broken heart and helping him see on a deeper, personal level how his soul loves, I could help him mend his broken heart. I hardly had to do any physical work on his heart as it related to any medical issue or effects from the heart attack. **Remember, the Law of Attraction is always at work, either for you or against you. It's your choice.**

There is one more point I would like to discuss as it relates to seeking an energy healer. I have often been asked, "How do I revive my chakras if I have been ignoring my spiritual self for so long?" You just answered the question for yourself. You realized that you've been ignoring your core. Once you start giving yourself the attention you deserve, you will be reviving your chakras. Reviving your chakras will create opportunities and synchronicity in your life.

As you start giving attention to your spiritual needs, the first question I would ask is, "Who am I?" I'm not talking about your name or what you do for a living. I'm talking about who you are as a spiritual being in the Universe. Who are you? I would ask myself that question every night, meditating on it as you fall asleep.

As you begin to realize who you are, how you're connected to infinite Divine Source and how you play an extraordinary role in the great cosmic dance, you revive your spiritual involvement. When you begin to understand that you are here for a purpose and that your life has meaning, your energy level will automatically start to change. Your beliefs will start to change and you will start to discover some of those nagging negative beliefs. They will come out because you are in an energetic place where you can rise above your negativity to clearly see them. You have the power to change limiting beliefs. If you can find every negative belief you have, had or will have, then you can write them down and convert them into positive ones. Meditate on the new positive beliefs, letting them permeate, not just for two minutes, but maybe during a long walk. Meditate on the new beliefs over and over and over again until they literally saturate every part of your consciousness. When that happens, the negative belief will be gone and you'll be able to move forward.

Start off by asking yourself, "who am I?" That query will get those chakras to open again because they respond to your thoughts more than anything else. I could literally work on your chakras for hours, but aside from using some form of tantric or breathing techniques, those chakras are going to stay wherever they are unless you change your inner dynamics and your inner beliefs. Remember, energy healers can help you heal, so long as you are willing to attract the healing to yourself.

CHAPTER 13: HYPNOSIS AND THE LAW OF ATTRACTION

"You create your own universe

as you go along."

Winston S. Churchill

Hypnosis is a scary word for some people. It is often associated with being under a spell where you are not in control of yourself. The word "hypnosis" might bring images of magic shows, carnivals, or exhibits at the fair. Whatever thoughts might come with the word hypnosis, there is no doubt that questions about it will follow. This chapter is about giving a broader, more defined understanding of what hypnosis is and how it relates to the Law of Attraction.

First off, let's begin with the Law of Attraction and the Emerald Tablet. I know that I have mentioned the Emerald Tablet many times throughout this book but it is the key element to the Law of Attraction. In fact, the Emerald Tablet was found to be the most prized object in the world by Alexander the Great. It was so precious and powerful to him that he hid the original stone. In fact, he hid it so well that, to this day, we still do not know where the original exists. Luckily for us, there were scribes who made copies of it. There are beliefs that the Tablet is supposedly written by Divine Source or Hermes, the great sage, who lived in Egypt. Archaeologist have no solid evidence as to where it came from.

Alexander believed that this document was so powerful that the secrets to this Emerald Tablet must be kept from common and uneducated people. Alexander knew that these secrets where the key to him conquering the known world at that time. The Emerald Tablet taught Alexander the Great that what he created above must manifest below. **When you create a vision on the higher plane of reality, it must manifest into your life.** Your creation manifests through direction, motion and commitment, followed by taking action toward the goal or desired outcome. When you take all of those steps, you see incredible miracles happen in your life. This was the knowledge implemented by Alexander the Great, who conquered the world.

Most people want to know that no matter what condition their lives are in, or whatever is going on, they can do something to make life more enjoyable, abundant and happy. You have the power to change your life anytime you desire. **You have the power to attract incredible, unbelievable health. You have the power to attract incredible, unbelievable wealth, happiness, love or anything else you desire according to the Emerald Tablet of Hermes.** You have the power to become a millionaire or a billionaire. You have the power to literally change your reality in incredible ways. **You can do this.** The Emerald Tablet of Hermes and the Law of Attraction give you a formula to make an attraction plan.

As I mentor clients all over the world, I sincerely enjoy the opportunity to empower so many different kinds of people from different backgrounds. In Miracle Mentoring and Alchemy Life

Coaching, the starting point is defining all the desires you expect to manifest in your life. It is important that you understand exactly what your goals are. Usually, the list of desires is very long and must be broken down into a few specific goals that will be focused on. The key is defining the desires that you are truly passionate about. It is common to discover that you have known what these desires were for quite some time. **Some of you knew or know that you are supposed to be doing something special with your life.** Many of you have known this since you were born. You have no doubt in your mind that there is an incredible wonder that you're called to accomplish with your life.

My job as a Miracle Mentor is to help you discover what you really desire to do; what you really desire to accomplish. If you don't know what you desire to accomplish then there's nothing I or anyone else can do for you. You need to know what kind of life you desire to live. That's the Law of Attraction! You must create it above first and know beyond any shadow of a doubt this is what you truly desire.

Sometimes, the problem is that people know what they desire, but they can't understand why they're not getting it. Some people think the Universe is out to get them, or they were born under an unlucky star. At times, there are negative energies in the Universe that must be confronted and dealt with. For these situations, I have a toolbox full of tools to use, including hypnosis and Miracle Magic. However, often what is thought to be negative energy is just counter-intentions interfering with your progress to manifest your desires. These are the intentions inside your subconscious mind that are pulling you in the opposite direction of your goals. Counter-intentions are sometimes created in childhood, as a teenager, or in some cases they were created in a past life. Yes, you read that correctly; in a past life. The funny fact is, don't have to believe in past lives to know that dealing with past life issues works.

For example, you may desire incredible health and vitality, but you're sick all the time. The question you have to ask is "why am I attracting this?" What are you doing in your subconscious? What is taking place in your subconscious mind that is attracting or empowering this chronic lack of health or whatever it is you desire? Hypnosis is a powerful technique utilized to talk to the subconscious mind.

The fact of the matter is, you can't just go to any hypnotherapist. Hypnotists are like postage stamps; they're all over the place. You need a hypnotist that understands the Law of Attraction and what you desire to accomplish. I personally believe that hypnotherapy done over Skype where you are laying in the comfort of your own home is far more effective than going into an office where you are always treated as guest. When you are in *your* environment, in your favorite lounge chair or in your bed with pillows propped behind you, the energy of the hypnosis work is not only affecting you, it is changing *your* environment. A downtown office is never your environment, so it's always artificial.

I believe that the choice of home hypnosis is preferred. Choosing to get in the car and driving across town to sit in an environment that is usually not very soundproof, does not keep most people in the optimal state of relaxation. It is a beautiful experience to pick a nice time of day when it's quiet in your home, sitting in your own recliner and making a Skype call to your hypnotist. I think you're far ahead by doing the work over Skype. My experience has shown that clients focus their concentration better at home. In the office, they never seem to get completely focused.

I still do hypnotherapy work out of an office along with my work over Skype. In the hypnotherapy office, people come in, sit in a recliner and they are guided into a relaxing trance. Clients will tell you that some remarkable breakthroughs occur in the office. My clients usually see results in two to five sessions. Hypnotic success can happen either place, but given the choice, in home hypnosis is much more powerful.

Hypnosis allows a discussion with the subconscious mind to get rid of counter-intentions and negative or limiting beliefs. In hypnosis, clients are clearing the roadblocks that have stopped them from taking actions and attracting the life they desire. Understand, what I do is not ordinary hypnosis; it is Law of Attraction hypnosis. That's why it is called "Miracle Hypnosis". **Once the blocks are gone the money flows, the love grows and the quality of life elevates.** It is hypnosis that uses the knowledge of the Emerald Tablet and the tools of Alchemy Life Coaching.

Hypnosis is not new. The ancients, Egyptians, Kabbalists, mystical Christians, pagans and others all used hypnosis. Understand that just sitting around the campfire and focusing on what you desire is a form of hypnosis. A woman called the other day and asked if it was possible to be hypnotized against her knowledge. I said, "Yes, it's called television commercials." I am sure you have seen a commercial for a new product or food and suddenly, you wanted the advertised product. If you hadn't seen and heard about it you would just go about your day without interruption. However, you now want something even though it may not be in line with your goals. This is a form of hypnosis.

We all go in and out of hypnosis all the time. **Hypnosis is just a relaxed state of focused concentration.** In a state of hypnosis the conscious mind is calm but the subconscious is very active, taking in new information or remembering old programing. During a Miracle Hypnosis session, the mind releases the old programing as it actively absorbs new information. Miracle Hypnosis counteracts the old programs or counter-intentions that rise up against your goals and desires. Counter-intentions are the antagonists against the dreams you desire to manifest. You seek all these positive changes like more money, better relationships, eliminating fears and better health, but you remain stuck. You try over and over again. You write out your goals or outcomes, use wish boards, repeat affirmations, say incantations, and use all the Law of Attraction tips you know, but you're still stuck. You are stuck because you have counter-intentions.

Miracles happen when hypnosis is done using the Law of Attraction. This style of hypnosis will help you with habits and behavioral changes. The changes that are taking place in hypnosis are on an unconscious level. Here you can eliminate unwanted habits, improve behavior, increase self-esteem, accelerate learning and remove anxiety. Can you imagine how nice it would feel not to be anxious? Can you imagine just feeling free flowing energy in your body, taking you to where you desire to go; bringing you joy, happiness, health and love?

This task of imagining is a type of hypnosis called creative visualization. Most people do not think of creative visualization as hypnosis. **Creative visualization is a powerful tool used to direct the subconscious mind like hypnosis.** Visualization takes place on a spectrum of different levels, not just during a hypnosis session.

In the creative visualization process, the goal is to maximize all of the senses: hearing, sight, smell, touch and taste. The key is to maximize your visualization process. **The clearer you visualize your goals, dreams and outcomes, the greater chance you have in gaining the inner knowledge and insight that leads you to manifest all that you desire.** Under the hypnotic aspects of creative visualization, you can literally feel opportunities come into your life. You will start to see offers and doors open that were not there before. You are creating according to the Emerald Tablet of Hermes. I witness this all the time in my hypnosis work during Miracle Mentoring and Alchemy Life Coaching. Alchemy means "going through changes"; *the level of transformation takes place in the deepest inner aspects of who you are.* Hypnosis is just one of the tools I use to start an alchemical chain reaction in someone's life.

There are many people that are trapped in the energy of being emotionally upset. I was with a friend recently who said he has part of his being that has been emotionally upset since childhood. Do you think that's helping him? Do you think that's empowering him in some way? This energy needs to be cleared out through hypnosis.

One of the lessons I teach is the skill of how to clear. In Miracle Hypnosis clients experience negative energy, emotional upsets, guilt, anger and grief all being cleared away. All of those negative states of consciousness that keep you from having the kind of life you desire are transformed into empowerment through hypnosis.

One aspect of emotional clearing is bringing your subconscious mind to a state of forgiveness. Forgiveness is not, "I will forgive but I will not forget." How many times have you heard people say that? True forgiveness is forgetting. It is allowing new empowering thoughts to rule the mind. I can tell you how to recognize if someone has forgiven. Ask yourself, "Do they keep bringing the issue up?" If they keep bringing it up, does that mean that they have forgiven? OF COURSE NOT! They have not forgotten, therefore, they did not forgive. **Forgiveness involves forgetting, letting it go and moving on.**

There is an epidemic of people in prison. It's absolutely crazy. There are people that don't need to be there. Many of these people had goals and dreams but were wounded by child abuse, sexual abuse, emotional pain and/or drugs. Most of these people never were given the knowledge or assistance to clear their mind and remove their counter-intentions. Through the power of Miracle Hypnosis, you can clear negativity and move through any negativity that, in extreme cases, might lead to prison. Miracle Hypnosis opens a path which allows you to flow into the next level of attracting the desires of your life as you leave the past behind. Hypnosis brings healing, strengthens your immune system, gets rid of repressed energies and programs your subconscious mind to be your ally rather than your enemy. Think about it. You have goals and dreams but you are your own worst enemy.

There is so much power in *true* Law of Attraction hypnosis. I regularly invoke hypnosis to control chronic pain. Hypnosis can reduce chronic pain because it teaches your mind how to be in control of your body's pain reaction. I have seen hypnosis bring about a smooth childbirth. Why not experience the joy of having a child without all the pharmaceutical drugs? You can have a wonderful birthing experience while being relaxed, aware and fully alert with Miracle Hypnosis.

The power of Miracle Hypnosis also assists in weight control. It's crazy how many people struggle to maintain a healthy body. Today's culture of abundant food and time consuming non-active responsibilities have made it easy to become overweight. In fact, society has made it almost acceptable to consume more than your share and be overweight. You walk down the street and the sidewalks are full of overweight people with hamburgers in their hands. I know that there's no fun in wanting to have a healthy vigorous lifestyle when you're overweight because the cravings are overwhelming. You feel like you're a slave to food. Miracle Hypnosis will aid you in dominating your craving and put you back in control of your life.

Maybe you suffer from cigarette cravings. Smoking and drug addiction keep you from attracting the dreams you really desire in life. In Miracle Mentoring and Alchemy Life Coaching, Miracle Hypnosis is used to diminish and destroy these cravings in the subconscious mind. Hypnosis does not stop with just diminishing cravings. It goes beyond diminishing cravings to start programing the subconscious to take action toward where you desire to go, what you desire to achieve, what you desire to own and who you desire to become. Miracle Hypnosis empowers you to create the kind of love you crave and earn the kind of money you deserve to make. Miracle Hypnosis touches all of these vital aspects of life.

If any information in this chapter has inspired you to look for a hypnotist to hire, check to see if they will teach you some forms of self-hypnosis. This is a great way to test the skills of your hypnotist. Only highly skilled and master hypnotists are willing to teach self-hypnosis techniques. After a few Miracle Hypnosis sessions, I like to teach clients how to put themselves into a deep relaxed state so they can literally reprogram their minds for maximum success. In just a few sessions, my client's mind knows how to enter the relaxed, reprogramming state of Miracle Hypnosis. It is then easy to teach the client's conscious mind to embed powerful life changing incantations into their subconscious mind. When the client can relax into opening up the subconscious mind, I can teach them the magnetic way to say magical incantations to direct new thinking patterns. This is the very ancient power of hypnosis put to practical use. This is one of the secrets of Miracle Hypnosis.

Do you own a business? Are you an artist? Do you have writer's block? Are you trying to build your business? Do you desire to release anger or cope with illness? Do you need some hypnotic anesthesia so you can visit the dentist? Are you dreaming about improving your work performance or speaking ability? Do you write out elaborate goals then procrastinate taking action? All of these issues are important. Powerful Miracle Hypnosis can resolve all these issues and more.

Everyone gets one shot at life. This is it; you're in *now time*. Some people say, "Well, I didn't get the owner's manual when I was born." There's no owner's manual. You can change your life now. You can do it in incredible ways. You can make progress in ways that you never realized were possible. You can overcome any obstacles. However, no matter how much you try to do it consciously, if you have negative emotions working inside you, you're stuck. Get to the next level with Miracle Hypnosis and the Law of Attraction.

Miracle Hypnosis Opportunities:

- Please write to lawofattractionsolutions@gmail.com to be referred to a Certified Miracle Mentor & Alchemy Life Coach trained in Miracle Hypnosis near you.

- I am currently creating several Miracle Hypnosis audio programs that you can download and listen to in the comfort of your own home. Visit www.lawofattractionsolutions.com for the current programs available for download in the store.

CHAPTER 14: MAGICAL EMPOWERMENT OF THE LAW OF ATTRACTION

"As above,

so below."

Emerald Tablet of Hermes

I know that the word magic brings many different thoughts to mind based on the experiences and exposure you have had in life. To some people, magic might mean all the wonder of Walt Disney. To others, magic might mean the creepy witch in the haunted house. You might think of Harry Potter when you hear the word magic. You might think of cauldrons and voodoo dolls when you hear the word magic. Strip away any thoughts that might be in your mind when you hear the word magic so that a true definition for magic might be obtained. **Magic is nothing more than the art and science of causing reality to conform to will.**

The definition of magic sounds a lot like the Law of Attraction. When the Law of Attraction is working for you, it is a form of doing magic for yourself. However, when the Law of Attraction is working against you, it is a sign that your beliefs and actions are working against you like black magic. Anything that stops you from reaching your highest potential is negative magic or negative attraction. **Being filled with negative energy hinders you and attracts exactly what you don't desire.** When your thoughts, actions, and Higher Self are in harmony with your goals and desires, there is absolutely nothing that can stop you from manifesting your dreams. This is the magic of the Law of Attraction: to cause reality to conform to will.

In this chapter you will learn some specific magical techniques and ideas that will empower you in creative ways. Some of you might be saying, "This is crazy. There is nobody else out there talking about the Law of Attraction as it applies to magic." Please keep an open mind. You don't have to be a magician to manifest with these techniques. As a matter of fact, I have met many magicians who are very bad at manifesting their desires. You would think it would be the other way around.

Magicians know the magical techniques of color correspondences, burning incense, using aromatherapy and calling on planets to attract certain kinds of energy. I have seen many magicians who perform those skills, but they have become very pragmatic in their work. There is a tendency with magicians to start questioning everything to the point where eventually nothing works. They almost become like an agnostic, questioning everything about faith. Magicians in the magical community who have lost their faith are often known to be very jealous and envious of people who engage in physical manifestation work, such as attracting abundance & prosperity.

Who are the individuals that are the true manifesting magicians of abundance? They are the people who keep it simple and understand how the Law of Attraction works. They are the people who don't undermine the attraction magic by having negative thoughts. They are the people who learn specialized knowledge and use it. They are the people who understand that everything is first created in the mind. Magicians don't always wear robes; some of them wear business suits like Henry Ford, Walt Disney, Bill Gates and others. These people understand how real magic works and have an empire to prove it. You can have your own empire too.

For example, let's say you are at an Olympic swimming pool. You decide that you have had enough practice diving and it is time for the high dive. You climb up the ladder feeling excited for your first high dive. You walk to the edge of the board feeling confident that you have the skills for this dive. You jump off. Now, half way between the board and the water you start doubting your ability. Your doubt causes you to lose your focus and form. The result is a huge, extremely painful belly flop. Recognizing your error, you try again. This time as you do a full dive, you maintain your confidence, and you glide smoothly into the water. If you're going to throw yourself into the water, there's no room for half a dive. **You will always attract exactly what you visualize.**

The same is true in magic, or the Law of Attraction, or whatever belief system you choose to work with. You must give any type of magic or belief a 100% chance to work. Understanding how the Law of Attraction works is the beginning. This Law of Attraction knowledge creates a solid foundation to build an empire. Whatever attraction techniques or beliefs you are learning, you can take it to the next level by studying energy, quantum physics, and magic.

What I am going to teach you will seem like rather simple

magic, but the whole idea is to keep it simple. People have built countries, businesses, and empires on simple philosophies. W. Clement Stone had one simple philosophy made up of just three words. Those three words were his entire mantra for building an organization that led him to become a billionaire. His mantra was, **"Do it now!"** No procrastination, just action; action followed by action, followed by action. If this man can build a billion dollar empire off three words, what can you do with two, four, or five words? You can create an empire the same way.

There's nothing stopping you from getting what you truly desire by applying a magical mantra. Magic is just the amplification of the mind; it's taking what the mind wants and amplifying it by using the natural energies and elements in the Universe. A mantra is just one of the many magical tools that will amplify any Law of Attraction work. Utilizing the tools and ways of magic will give you an advantage that perhaps you haven't had in the past.

Many Law of Attraction gurus will let you know that you need to visualize and emotionalize all your Law of Attraction goals. Visualizing is a very important step in attracting, but the magic of letting go pushes it to the next level. In the magical concept of "letting go" or "giving it up to the Universe", you remove yourself from the state of need or want. You have to be able to look at your visualized and emotionalized goal and say, "I am attracting my goal free from a sense of desperation." For some reason, the Universe seems to act in a more powerful way when you aren't in a state of need, want, or desperation. **Understand that the attitude of "want" implies a state of lack.** Lack means you don't have it; it is outside of your grasp. The

Universe picks up on the subconscious message in your mind "that you don't have" *instead* of the fact that you "are focused on attracting your desire".

One of my hobbies is horse racing. I like horse racing but I don't NEED it. Winners come one after the other when you are not desperately needing a win. The basic premise is that it is always easier to attract money when you have money because you are not in a state of need or want. This is how the magic of letting go works to amplify the Law of Attraction. I was at the track not too long ago and I threw down a six-dollar bet and won 600 dollars. I wasn't intently focused on winning, I simply thought that I would like to win, then I let it go. The Universe understood that I sent out the call to win, I had a picture of what I wanted, and then I moved on and focused on enjoying my day at the race track. By stepping out of the way, I allowed the energy to flow more freely. That's the key to real magic and the Law of Attraction.

When you send an intention out into the Universe, you will be more productive saying, "I have this already, I'm feeling good about it." In the mentoring work I do, I use what I call "Miracle Magic" to activate a client's attraction abilities. I use special techniques to change the energy field of the client because the client is not yet resonating at a high enough vibration to allow the client to change his or her own energy field. A few of these clients end up calling me every day saying, "Robert, it's not working yet." Guess what? It's not working because you're sitting by the phone worrying about whether it's working. **Relax and let the Universe do the work for you.**

The power is in the Universe. The power is in the intention. The first part of any good magical act is to have a well-formed intention. What's your intention? What do you intend accomplish or attract? What are you transforming in your life? Do you desire more money, a better job, a better relationship, or career advancement? Let's use the desire for a career advancement as an example.

You can't approach attracting a career advancement as if it's something you don't have. You must see the career advancement as something you *already have* and it's just a matter of timing. Then as you begin to visualize, it's important to activate all the sub-modalities. Visual senses mean you have to see it. When you want to activate the sensation of feeling, you have to be able to touch an object with your hands. Activate your auditory senses; what does your goal sound like? You could hear the sound of money going into your pocket, or a check being written out for a million dollars! That's what Jim Carrey did. He would carry a fake check made out to him for 20 million dollars. Jim Carrey would see it, feel it, touch it and let it go each time he opened his wallet. He knew it would happen; it was just a matter of time.

No matter what your goal, you must be willing to let it go. Let the Universe do the work for you. You can't hold onto it by stubbornly saying incantations and complaining that your goal is not manifesting faster. This is just operating out of the ego or having a temper tantrum. You're not going to attract what you desire when you're operating *only* from the will part of your brain. You have to operate out of your subconscious mind, which is the connecting link to the entire Universe. Visualization is an extremely powerful form of mental magic. There's not a businessman or woman in the world that doesn't shut his or her eyes and visualize what he or she desires. Engage in the mental magic of creative visualization, then let the Universe go to work for you. Do it now.

Let's talk about a specific magical way to employ color. Including vivid colors in your creative visualization will activate your subconscious mind, thus giving your visualization more luster and life. I'm going to give you a basic color outline after this example.

Let's say you're a college student working on your Ph.D. paper and you're really struggling. First, stop struggling. Take a deep breath and RELAX. Then, do some creative visualization. See every sentence forming exactly as you want it while you are writing. As you visualize, see the words in bright orange. Watch the whole paper turn bright orange. I know you are asking, "Why orange?" On the Kabbalistic Tree of Life, *orange is the color of Hod.* Hod is the emanation on the Tree of Life containing the energy of the expression of the left-brain. Hod also holds a relationship to the planet Mercury. Mercury is the fastest spinning planet, which represents the intellect. Now, take your visualization beyond your paper. Visualize your entire workstation in orange. Make your attire orange, make the trees outside the window orange, make the campus buildings orange, and even make your Professor orange. This is the magic of color visualization. Focusing the vibrational energy of the appropriate color on your situation and goal will amplify your attraction power. You are not likely to find this is the kind of magical information in any other book on the Law of Attraction. Checkout some basic color as they relate to the elements.

Yellow is the color of Air. The element of Air represents the vibration of the mind, thoughts and ideas. Are you having brain fog, or is your mind overflowing with negative thoughts? Clear it up with Air and the color yellow.

Red is the color of Fire. It is the power and passion for life. Get fired up! If you can't get motivated, Fire is exactly what you need. You will be amazed at the passion acquired from a simple red glass candle mediation. Begin by lighting some big red glass candles in the room where you meditate. Set the lit candles at eye level, if possible. Now allow your eyes to gaze in, around, and through the light. As your gaze relaxes into the flame, let your mind drift off. Allow the flame to melt all the limiting thoughts out of your mind. Limiting thoughts keep ideas from flowing naturally. Allow your mind to slowly transition into visualizing all that your heart desires. Perhaps you desire your boyfriend back. See him coming into your life, calling you on a red phone and you answer the red phone as you sit on a red couch. You can change the color of any object in your mind. That's the beautiful phenomenon about having a brain; you have the power to control your mind! What this exercise has done is attract the element of Fire into your visualization. The Fire mixes with your energy field so that after a day or two you will realize that your motivation level has increased. You will experience passion swirling around your situation. It's absolutely astonishing how much Fire a little red visualization will add to your goals being attracted.

Blue is the color of water. Go look at the ocean. You will notice when you're on the ocean in a boat, inner tube, or surfboard that you are unable to experience what is beneath you. The ocean has unknown depth. Water is about depth; deep emotional depth. Imagine the kind of emotional depth you can create for yourself through the Law of Attraction by visualizing your goals and dreams in blue. Blue can also transform the ways you desire the world to feel about you. Understand that you never have the ability to take away free will, but you do have the ability to enhance your energy field and the field of those around you. Basically, what you are doing is switching from a black and white TV to a color TV. If you desire more depth, surround yourself with blue while coloring your entire visualization in blue.

Green, especially dark green, is the color of Earth. Green is always about wealth, prosperity, and abundance. Green also represents sowing and reaping. You can use green energy by taking a green piece of paper; write your intention on it and looking at it every day. Set your intention, visualize it, meditate on it and see yourself moving into that new house, or acquiring a pay raise, or whatever it is that you desire that relates to material success. Visualize it all in green. There's a reason why money is primarily green in this country. If you desire financial stability, use a nice dark green color. Unlock abundance with magical green energy.

Let me share one more magical attraction technique. Most that have studied the Law of Attraction know about using dream or vision boards. A dream board is an amazing tool to help you attract what you desire by taking your visualizations to a tangible level. How about covering your dream boards (yes, you might want to have more than one) in the color that can help you get what you desire? If you desire a car and it has to be silver, cut out a picture of that silver car and put it on your dream board with a dark green piece of construction paper as the background. Colors operate at different vibrations. Use magical colors with the Law of Attraction to empower yourself as you manifest the life you desire.

There are many more magical techniques I use from my years of ancient studies. Several methods not published anywhere are used in my Miracle Mentoring and Alchemy Life Coaching practice. The colors I used in this chapter are from the Esoteric Order of the Golden Dawn. (www.esotericgoldendawn.com)

This is your life. Your choice now is to make it magical and enjoyable. Knowing what you desire and going after it is only a portion of what is necessary to get it. Developing the inner and magical tools to create the life you desire will give you a significant edge as you manifest your goals.

CHAPTER 15: THE FOUR ELEMENTS AND THE LAW OF ATTRACTION

"So I say to you: Ask and it will be given to you;

seek and you will find;

knock and the door will be opened to you."

Jesus Christ

What is the Law of Attraction? What is it about? Where is it all from? Many years ago, in Egyptian times, the Ancients believed the god Tehuti came down and inscribed for them the secret and sacred teachings on the Emerald Tablet. Some people attribute the Emerald Tablet to the sage Hermes, but nobody can authenticate the author's identity. What is known is that all the ancient mystery schools, including mystic Christianity and the teachings of Jesus, were based on the Law of Attraction. This teaching is summed up in the phrase, "As above, so below." **In other words, what you create in your mind will eventually manifest in reality.**

You attract whatever you think. It doesn't mean you can't have a thought that is contrary to what you desire. In fact, you probably will entertain counter-intentions. Science has proven in recent years that there is an antagonistic part of our brain that is designed to challenge your deepest beliefs. However, you can control what you do with these antagonistic thoughts. Critical thinking requires both positive and negative thoughts. When counter-thoughts become dominant, they become emotionalized and take on a life of their own. You start giving negativity legs to walk all over your dreams. These counter-intentions that are taking you in the opposite direction of where you desire to go are often based on fears or anxieties. Not the kind of anxiety where you are shaking in a complete panic attack, but the type of anxiety where you feel a sense of impending doom or nervousness about the day ahead. When you are living an extraordinary life you wake up early in the morning and can't wait to get out of bed because you are so excited about your life. When you are excited about the things you can create, teach, learn and feel, you are sending positive energy through the Universe. When you're excited about life, when you're excited about what you desire to do, then you are invoking the corresponding predominant energy and emotions attached to your goal.

I believe that all emotions spring forth initially from thought. You have a thought and it is given life through your emotions, or it just passes away without emotions given to it. **Thoughts and goals receive animation through your emotions.** This is why emotionalizing your goals empowers your capacity to attract. Your ability to emotionalize grants everything a magnetic attracting force. The Emerald Tablet reveals this truth. Most can easily understand this concept of emotionalizing when watching a negative thought. Everyone knows from experience what happens when you focus on situations you don't desire. You immediately start emotionalizing through fear and anxiety; you create a list of a thousand "what ifs" that would "destroy you". When you have a negative thought, let it go without attaching

145

emotions to it. Simply say, "Cancel that thought" followed immediately by a positive, affirming thought. Counterbalance negativity and manifest desired outcomes with strong, positive, emotions.

The goals you desire to attract are the goals you think about the most. It is also the goals you emotionalize the most. In other words, you have an energetic attachment to those thoughts, visions and pictures. Your dominant thoughts will find a way to manifest because like attracts like. It's pretty simple. When Einstein worked on his theory of relativity, there were pieces that he could comprehend completely and pieces that he could not yet comprehend. Einstein stuck with it, thinking about relativity day and night. Eventually, he reached the point where he began to visualize his theories and the more he visualized them, the more he understood. The emotional energy he sent into the Universe returned to him as knowledge that manifested as a theory and a mathematical formula.

Think of anyone who is known for great accomplishments. Nelson Mandela, for example, was in prison for 27 years, but his thinking sparked visualizations in others that increased a level of understanding that manifested change in our modern world. What do you think was in his mind all that time in prison? The only thought he had in his mind was what he would accomplish when he got out of prison. Nelson Mandela did not focus on the gloom of prison. Instead, he emotionalized the glory of freedom and how he could change his country and the world. It's very important to take responsibility for the thoughts that you think because your thoughts attract the situations that materialize in your life.

You will find that the opportunities you attract seem to appear like magic. There are many different ways of creating a magnetic attraction reaction. I use the ancient ideas of attraction along with modern science to empower my attraction techniques. You can read attraction teachings over and over, but they can't sink deep into your mind if you entertain counter-intentions at the same time. You often need another to guide you through looking at all your counter-intentions to help yourselves eradicate them. My Miracle Mentoring and Alchemy Life Coaching clients are guided into the depths of their subconscious mind to surgically remove those counter-intentions. Counter-intentions, negative thoughts, old scars, beliefs from your upbringing, call it what you want, but this is what is keeping you from your dreams. It all must be eradicated from your thinking process because it is hindering your attraction.

The ancients understood the concept of the microcosm and the macrocosm. What is the microcosm? The ancients often defined the microcosm through symbols, particularly with the symbol of the Pentagram. Let me explain the true meaning of the Pentagram as the ancients understood it. This is a very different meaning from the modern and exaggerated Hollywood definition of the pentagram.

The Pentagram symbolizes the four elements, with Spirit ruling above, in the macrocosm. It is an image like a star where the top point represents Spirit pouring down into the other four points, which represent the four elements. The Pentagram can also be seen as a man with his arms and legs outstretched. In the symbol of the man, each hand and foot represents one of the four elements with Spirit above. The arms and legs have no life on their own until Spirit pours down into them.

In Neurolinguistic Alchemy, there is a spiritual presupposition that traditional neurolinguistic programming does not have. In Alchemy, there is a total understanding that everything functions by Spirit flowing through the four elements. The four elements are Air, Fire, Water and Earth brought to life, of course, by Spirit. I believe that is not my responsibility to define Spirit, for Spirit is beyond human comprehension. It's up to you to find your own definition and spiritual practice that works for you. Your own understanding of Spirit must be accompanied by an understanding of the four elements. You will be at a loss of how to use the Pentagram without an understanding of the four elements. The Spirit works together with the elements. As you evoke the nature of each element, you empower the Law of Attraction in your life. Let me share a brief understanding of each element and its influences within you.

Air is an active element. It's moving and hardly ever still. It relates to intellect, ideas and movement. In relation to finances, Air represents opportunities opening up. It can blow away old ideas and beliefs to bring in new life and energy. Air awakens opportunity in your life. This quality of Air allows miracles to happen when using the Law of Attraction. You may desire to attract great wealth, but if you don't have the opportunity, attracting money will be difficult. Air can give you that opportunity. Learning how to awaken the element of Air empowers your application of the Law of Attraction to work with opportunities. Air will move you in the right direction toward your goals.

Fire is important because it deals with passion. Passion is the energy of life. Show me someone who isn't passionate about who they are and I will show you someone who is leading a boring and unhealthy life. Passionless people are just not happy. They look at life as having a job, having recreation time, with every activity separated from who they are. Passionless people don't look at life as fulfilling a mission, a purpose or being a piece of a greater picture. In the eyes of the passionless, life has no tangible importance. I think that people learning to use the Law of Attraction believe their lives have value and purpose. Passionate people see life as more than just sitting back. The power of passion alone is enough to give you a sense of power.

I will take the individual who has passion over the person who has skills. Skills alone are not enough. Skills give you the tools, but passion gives you the momentum. Skills and passion work very well together, almost like Sun and Moon.

Fire also holds the power of purification. It really symbolizes purifying all of those negative thoughts out of your sphere of sensation to allow passion to rise. Fire purifies all of those thoughts that are counter to what you're trying to attract. Did the ancients have it right? Of course they did. They knew that a priest had to be purified before he went into the Holy of Holies. Do you have some negative beliefs that you want to eradicate? You must get rid of negative intentions. You have to be purified. Fire is the agent by which you can be purified.

Fire can influence your financial state. Fire gives you the passion to attract the money to see your dreams actualized. It's a desire to earn more money to expand your reach. It is a desire to help the homeless, to feed the poor, or expand the ways you pay it forward. Every bird has a song to sing and every human has a dream to actualize. Attracting a financial increase will increase the volume of your song. When you reach that point where you say, "I will die if I cannot sing my song", then passion of Fire will burn away the obstacles you could come across, even if it is financial.

Water contains the influence of higher emotions. If the goals you seek to attract are just lower wishes, you are not invoking the Law of Attraction. As a matter of fact, lower wishes often work against you because you don't believe those lower wishes can be achieved. When your higher emotions are driving your actions, then your goals are filled with the element of Water. Water reveals higher emotion and higher purpose. It's not just about increase of income, it's about increase of income so my children can go to school, so my wife and I can travel, and the like.

Water is also about money flow. Think of money as a paddle wheel. If you're hoarding money, there is not an opening for more money to flow. Money that does not flow is evidence that you've established a belief system that money is hard to come by. Imagine what a belief system would be like if you really believed that money was easy to come by. Sure, there may be times when money does not flow as easily, and I'm not telling you to be careless with your money, but let your money flow even in leaner times. Let money do what you desire it to do. Now that you're attracting the money, why not let it flow? Why not throw yourself into the river and let your life flow? Don't hold yourself back from being your best.

Water is also an influence of intuition. Intuitive people just "know that they know." These are people that go it alone and go against the crowd. Then one day, the loner becomes the new crowd leader because they develop a new way and flow with Water.

Earth holds the power of self-identity. Within the element of Earth, who you are and your grounded-ness is found. Earth is your foundation. It deals with your fertility. This is not just "having children" fertility, but also a fertile life experience. It's about who you really are. Earth is about organization and everything in the right place at the right time. Earth is about abundance and famine. Look at people on the Earth. One plot of soil produces an abundant amount of food, while the other plot produces nothing. You have to pay attention to what kind of Earth you are invoking. It's about invoking the fertility of Earth under the ray of spring or fall. Spring is when you take action. It's the law of the harvest and planting new seeds. You've always got to be planting new seeds. Fall is when you harvest. This means putting yourself in a position to accept these opportunities. Earth is about sowing seeds and reaping harvest.

I like the idea of using a vision board, or two, or three. I've seen so many people find success through a vision board. Miracles are accelerated with vision boards, especially Pentagram vision boards. The Pentagram vision board is a powerful tool used to put every item being attracted in a section according to the element that will assist in manifesting it. So assess where you are in the process of attracting each goal and be clear about what you want. Look to see which element you need to invoke to get your goal closer to manifestation. Do this by analyzing the qualities of each element and see what kind of energy you need. For example, examine the concept of stagnation. If you're feeling stagnant, invoke Water. Find out why you are feeling the stagnation and ask how to get the river flowing again. If your situation seems shaky, look at the element of Earth. You can use the four elements to help you manifest the kind of goals that you desire through the Law of Attraction. The Pentagram is a powerful elemental tool of attraction.

For more information on the Pentagram, I would suggest our book on healing called, Magical Energy Healing: The Ruach Healing Method. It is available on Amazon and Barnes and Noble. I also like the book Modern Magick by the late Donald Michael Kraig. You can learn more information on our websites:

www.lawofattractionsolutions.com

and

www.esotericgoldendawn.com.

CHAPTER 16: THE POWER OF ANGELS AND THE LAW OF ATTRACTION

"Whether you think you can,

or you think you can't –

you're right,"

Henry Ford

I generally talk about the Law of Attraction and many other related subjects from the perspective of ancient studies. The Ancients held untold treasures that revolve around the Law of Attraction. Once you have an understanding of these untold treasures, you can apply them to your life. Ancient studies can be used today to empower the kind of Law of Attraction results that you should get, that you expect to get and that you deserve to get.

One of these ancient studies is an understanding of the power of angels. How can the power of angels help you in your life? How can angels help invoke the kind of life you desire, vitality you require, relationships you build, prosperity you share, and lands you explore? In this chapter, I will give an overview of my understanding of the power of angels. Let me make it clear that one chapter can only scratch the surface of the topic of angels. You can spend a lifetime dedicated to understanding angels.

Angels go as far back as anyone can remember. Angels are a

part of almost every mystery tradition. They are referred to as energies, gods or angels throughout ancient documents. Whatever word is used to describe angels, they are Divine energetic emanations from a Divine Supernatural Spiritual Source. The earliest writings from ancient Egypt, Persia and India speak of "winged beings" or "messengers of God". In various traditions such as Kabbalah, mystical Christianity and the Angels of Enochian, there are writings about a variety of angelic hierarchies. Angels are mentioned in the Bible, the Torah and the Koran. For example, the great Archangels Gabriel and Michael, both appear in the Old and New Testaments of the Bible. Raphael appears in the Book of Tobit. Uriel/Ariel appears in the writings of Enoch. Perhaps the richest source of angel lore is the Holy Kabbalah itself. In Kabbalah, angel lore is specifically found in the Book of Zohar, also known as the Book of Splendor. The Sepher Yetzirah, which is known as the Kabbalistic Book of Formation, gives a great understanding of angels as well. Along with all these books, there are several ancient hermetic writings that contribute to an understanding of angels. These writings are studied in mystery schools like the Esoteric Order of the Golden Dawn.

Here's one interesting fact I want to get across right from the beginning. Angels both give and receive messages or energy. It is absolutely imperative that this is understood. Often, angels are just thought of as messengers from the Divine Source. Angels can also be messengers to Divine Source. Angels can deliver inspiration. When you open up to angelic forces, you will have more ideas and more energy to accomplish your goals. Manifesting your dreams will be easier than you've ever imagined possible. Angels can also take your inspired ideas to Divine Source to create a path of execution for the idea. Angels work both ways. Think of Jacob's Ladder, where the angels climb up and down from Divine Source to the earthly realm (Genesis 28:12). Angels become a powerful vehicle for taking our intention, transferring it, empowering it, adding passion, giving it energy and juice, then bringing it to Divine Source. In the presence of the Divine, human intention is received and then brought back down to be manifested with the assistance of angels.

Let's get practical for a moment. Take the example of needing a new car. Which angel would you invoke? You have already set an intention for a new car and made a vision board featuring the car you desire. Now, it is time to ask for help from a specific force. There could be a number of angels that would be appropriate to invoke help from. In fact, there are thousands of angels; picking just one could be difficult. The deeper you study the power of angels and the mystery traditions, the more specific help you will invoke. From a practical standpoint, the Angel Uriel rules over the Earth and over the material world. What this means is that all the angels who come under Uriel's guidance or work with Uriel, would be appropriate to invoke and assist in obtaining your goal of a new car. The average person does not understand all the angels under Uriel so it is best to ask for aid from an arch or lead angel. Start your journey with angels by familiarizing yourself with the main Archangels.

When you desire to connect with an angel be sure to turn off any electronic devices like your cell phone and TV. Next, internally connect by simple saying "Uriel, I seek your assistance in materializing my intention of a new car." **After inflaming that**

intention with visualization, passion, and certainty, turn it over to Uriel. Let Uriel, through his sacred duty, bring that intention to Divine Source. Trust completely that, as Divine Source receives the seed of your intention, it will be brought into manifestation in the physical world. Expect your new car to come through the unexpected and mysterious ways of the Universe. You will find that, in a short period of time, money comes into your life to buy a car, or someone doesn't need a car and is willing to give you one, or you win a random drawing for a car. Divine Source has no limits in how the angels work in the Universe.

There is no point in asking a million questions about how angels empower your intention. Angels work on a quantum level which is beyond human comprehension. **You don't even need to believe in angels for them to be effective in helping you manifest your desires. Nobody knows for sure what angel energy is or how it works, or if it has wings, but it is a fact that the Universe seems to act as if they are real.**

I have been studying, working with and teaching about angels for over thirty-five years. In all my years, I come back to the Kabbalistic writings and ancient mystery traditions that seem to connect the way angels work with the Law of Attraction. Time and time again, it has been proven that angels have the ability to take your intention to the next level. They magnify the best of your goals. Angels are exceptionally powerful because they are emanations of God at different levels of manifestation.

Even with all the power that angels hold, the power of creation is only given to humans. Angels do not have the ability to create. Think about this for a moment. **Angels find their purpose in fulfilling the intent of Divine Source.** You are made in the image of the Divine; you are made as a creator. You have powerful energetic helpers in the creative process called "Angels".

Now, here's where it all gets very exciting. Where is Divine Source? Where is God? Where is this Infinite Light? Is it millions and billions and trillions of miles away? Or is it inside you? It states in the invocation of Tehuti, **"He is in me and I am in him."** That means that the Divine Source is in you and you are co-creator with the infinite. You are the microcosm of the macrocosm. **The Universe is in you.**

Your oneness with the Divine also means that all of the powerful heavenly beings, like the incredible Archangels and angels, live within you. The impact of this is ASTONISHING! Understanding your oneness empowers you with an exceptional creative force.

There are millions of ways that you can connect with angels to receive their assistance. One of the most effective ways of connecting with angels is using the Power of Angles program (Available at: www.lawofattractionsolutions.com). The beautiful, empowering music takes you into a deep meditation where you enter **"The Hall of Angels"**. This is a place where you present your intentions to the angels for aid and empowerment. It is great for those beginning angel work because you don't even have to know what is appropriate. In the Hall of Angels, all you have to do is have an intention written in a positive way and the right angel will grasp it right out of your heart.

The angel will disclose your goal to Divine Source and aid the manifestation of it in your life. Believe it, trust it, and be certain about it.

As you are taken into the Hall of Angels, absolutely astonishing invocations of Raphael, Uriel, Gabriel, and Michael transform your energy field. In ancient traditions, these are the archangels associated with the four elements and directions. **Raphael** is the Guardian Angel of the *East* and the Elemental Angel of *Air*. **Uriel** is the Guardian Angel of the *North* and the Elemental Angel of *Earth*. **Gabriel** is the Guardian Angel of the *West* and the Elemental Angel of *Water*. **Michael** is the Guardian Angel of the *South* and the Elemental Angel of *Fire*. Michael is a very powerful angel who carries a sword to cut away the qualities and situations in your life that do not serve your wellbeing. All angels, even personal Guardian Angels, can help you create by removing unnecessary obstacles in life. They can help you cut out the patterns that are holding you back from your true desires.

When you begin making contact with angels, particularly specific angels, you begin to absorb those angelic attributes for yourself and into your relationships. Each angel acts as an aspect of the Divine allowing the Divine spark within you to be activated. As you build angelic relationships, it's like any relationship, any friend you have, the more time you spend with them, the closer and more endeared you become. You can really empower your life by developing a deep personal relationship with angels. I remember when I began, the idea of even speaking with just one angel on a daily basis was so exhilarating. As I think back over the years, I am astonished when I realize how many angels I communicated with and know by name. As you are introduced to more and more angels, there are some that you will communicate with by in-depth conversation and others more as acquaintances.

Each angel has been given certain duties in the Universe. As you learn these duties, you can develop a camaraderie with the angels. This camaraderie will engage the angels in helping you achieve your goals and dreams by magnifying the power of the Law of Attraction in your reality. Angels will also help you to develop a more intimate relationship with Divine Source or God. Soon you will realize that everyone has angels influencing their lives every day, in so many different ways. Angels influence the successes and achievements that you are having, but only to a point. Remember, if you don't take responsibility for your part to fine tune and hone your ability to better communicate with angels, then there will be difficulty in manifesting your goals. You must continuously show that you are committed to taking action on the paths the angels help you create. It all really starts with your intention and desires. Angels then assist in transforming your life as you take action.

When working with angels, it is ultimately Divine Source working through you in your partnership to co-create the life you desire. You are still the author of your life, but these angels that you work with inspire you or open your mind in a way that perhaps wouldn't be possible if you weren't working with these angels.

It's interesting that people in the creative world often have no problem thinking about working with angels. In fact, they tend to have a natural connection and rapport with one specific angel. This angel is usually their Holy Guardian Angel. Creative individuals know that Divine Source is within them as they create through and with the help of their angel. They have a deep understanding of the Law of Attraction; often without knowing it. Angels, Divine Source, the Law of Attraction and *YOU* are all tied together.

In my years of mentoring clients all over the world, I have found that people don't usually think of angels when it comes to money. Money is usually associated with hard work. I am here to tell you that I have seen people work with angels who literally put thousands and thousands of dollars in their bank account. Money is just a creation tool like a paintbrush. When you ask angels to help you attract money to further your dreams and goals, miracles happen. I have seen people buy houses that they shouldn't have been able to buy. I am not talking about getting money through some shady loan program, but they were able to come up with the loan or the money in some unusual way. This is because invoking angels for help attracting the loan they needed gave them new hope. A positive trusting attitude in the angels will always increase your attraction power.

Let me give you an example. There was a gentleman that went to a Power of Angels workshop several years ago. I had not been in contact with him for years but he just called out of the blue. He explained how he had an intention and had been working with the angels I taught him about years ago. He told me about how he started working with these angels because he needed money for his children. He did not know how he would get the money but he trusted that the angels would assist his request. He could not believe it when he got a letter in the mail stating that he inherited a safety deposit box at the bank with $5,000 in it. Can you guess how much money he needed? It was exactly $5,000.

You might believe angels will never help you because you have some limiting beliefs or lack of understanding. If this is you, know that all you have to understand is that angels are energy from God. They are aspects of the Divine Source at a lower vibration available to assist you when you ask. It is important also to understand that money is an aspect of the Divine Source. Money is energy too, and it is hardly good for anything except giving you energy to further your dreams.

What about relationships? Angels can play such a marvelous, astonishing role in building powerful, lasting, loving, passionate relationships. The Archangel Gabriel can create an intuition between two people where they just know what each other needs. Gabriel can help relationships come to a place were a couple just knows what they want. It's almost as if they don't need to talk to each other. Michael can give them passion by cutting away all beliefs and situations that hinder the relationship. Michael will replace the strenuous and unimportant with passion, power, determination and will.

Raphael can bring harmony and healing to a relationship. Each person thinks a little bit differently. It is Raphael who can take our naturally inharmonious minds and harmonize our thinking so that our language and communication are in sync. You know the old saying of "men are from Mars and women are from Venus", so therefore they can't communicate. Invoke Raphael and suddenly the Divine Source starts working through Raphael to attract communication in your relationship. Angels are an unbelievably exciting key to your Law of Attraction success.

So, let me review the four main Archangels. For the physical material needs in your life, call on Uriel. For the assistance you need for the mind and healing, call on Raphael. For intuition and deeper emotional needs, call on Gabriel. When you need power, might, will, determination, and fortitude, call on Michael. These four Archangels and you create an absolutely incredible unstoppable team!

Napoleon Hill talks about these aspects in his book, "Think and Grow Rich", as his mastermind technique. Very simply, the mastermind technique is a way of calling on the energies of others to guide and help you. Why not create a mastermind group full of angelic emanations from Divine Source? When you call on an angelic mastermind, you can create anything you desire. There is nothing that you cannot attract into your life when you invoke angels with the Law of Attraction. (To get involved in deep angelic studies, join the Esoteric Order of the Golden Dawn at www.esotericgoldendawn.com.)

Chapter 17: Evil Spells, Black Magic and the Law of Attraction

"Peace comes from within.

Do not seek it without."

Buddha

I would like to share my knowledge about evil forces, negative forces, evil energy, black magic, and evil spirits as it relates to the Law of Attraction. I don't know of any other Law of Attraction coach that speaks on this subject, but in my many years of esoteric studies I have gathered a vast amount of knowledge on the subject. Every day, people call me saying, "Robert, I need some help. I've been setting goals and taking action to improve the quality of my life *but* nothing is working. It seems the harder I try, the worse the situation becomes. It seems like I have a spirit or something working against me." Sometimes people are direct and say, "I have a problem, I know my ex-wife has put a curse on me!"

This sounds outrageous to some of you, however it's not as outrageous as you might think. Years ago, it was more common to be attacked by black magic if you lived in Southern California, New York City, New Orleans or Florida. Today it has become prevalent everywhere with black magic practitioners for hire on the internet for as little as five dollars! At that rate, if you hired 10 people to do negative magic and even if none of them were skilled practitioners, there would still be enough low vibration energy sent into the Universe to cause an effect. **Remember, thoughts are things.** These practitioners are creating in the above to manifest negativity in the world below.

Desperate people, who do not understand how to focus on their own goals, spend time and energy trying to remove their pain by causing pain in the lives of others. These are the ones that seek out hiring a black magician, negative energy manipulator, or a dark arts practitioner to do negative or low vibratory magic. The desperate person may be trying to draw a lover back, win a lawsuit, destroy a disliked employer, or get revenge in some way. The good news is that there are specific Law of Attraction actions that can be taken to counteract and repel this type of energy. I have seen remarkable results as clients take action to build an attraction shield against negative forces.

Here's the challenge. You have to find out what your counter-intentions to your goals are and remove them. **Counter-intentions are the thoughts in your mind that act like black magic on your dreams.** If you don't remove and clear them completely, they will grow stronger. For example, say you desire to buy a new house but every time you get close to that positive intention, something bad or crazy happens to prevent you from getting the house. Maybe, the day before closing someone loses a job; wild, crazy stuff that only seems to happen to you. After a while, you may determine that there is some force keeping you from getting a house. It could simply be a counter-intention that is acting in the form of casting black magic on yourself.

There is no magician in the world more powerful than your own mind filled with counter-intentions. Your thoughts create things. As you think above, so it manifests below. Your counter-intention might appear as, "How will I ever keep up with my mortgage payments?", or "What if I don't like my neighbors?", or "What if I see a better house after I buy this one?" If you are spending any time emotionalizing thoughts like these, then you are casting black magic on yourself.

The other possibility is there are ill intentions from others being focused on you. For example, maybe friends are jealous of you buying a new house so they are focusing negative thoughts on you. Maybe your friends are subconsciously feeding you doubts as they talk to you about getting a house. Your parents might say that you are moving too far away. Your friends might say that you won't want to go out anymore. Guess what is happening? You've already got a breach in the dam and those negative thoughts are getting bigger and stronger as you move closer to buying a new house.

People's thoughts, when they are magnified, emotionalized and focused for a length of time, can have an enormous effect on your life. If you have counter-intentions in your subconscious mind, or a breach, which allows others to influence you, then there is an open door that allows black, dark, or negative energy to come through. Changing your thoughts and beliefs builds a shield against unwanted forces. When your belief system says "you are always in power, you are always in control," then you are the master of your life and all negative forces are repelled.

It's not about what happens in your life; unfortunate events happen in everybody's life! When researchers studied the people who survived the concentration camps of WWII, those people were found to have been the ones who always believed that they were in control of their own destiny. So, when your goal is planted deep in your subconscious mind, there is nothing that can come against you - not even negative forces or evil spirits. **You are bullet proof.** The problem is that most of us, through our childhood, learned some forms of helplessness and weakness. **You may have learned that being a victim from time to time is beneficial.** This provides a doorway for negative thoughts, jealousy and anger from other people to come into our lives.

Evil energy is when someone has taken the time to invoke some negative unwanted force. Whether it is a friend, magician or even a religious prayer group, they have actually wished consciously and subconsciously for ill will to be brought upon you. There has been an energetic force created against you. Sometimes, dark spirits are attracted to the manifestation energy in your life. In other words, if you're trying to achieve several goals in your life, dark spirits may feed off your energy. It is like they are picking up energetic crumbs from the floor that are now dirty and trying to mix it with your clean energy. If you are an achiever, you have to train your subconscious mind to be bullet-proof so you mentally repel negativity.

What about those who are known to be black magic practitioners from deep in the jungle of Africa or New Orleans? Many people I know do not believe in magic, let alone black magic. **Even if you don't believe in black magic, the Universe acts as if it's real.**

Why? It is because, at an energetic level, we're all connected together. Those that have a deep belief in dark arts are part of the spider web or matrix of thought with people who do not believe in dark arts. So, if a person or a trained individual pulls on one little point of that spider web, it will alter the entire web. If they focus their intention on harm, it can have an effect.

How does dark energy have an effect on those trying to achieve their goals? Evil magic, negative energy, dark forces and the like will always work on the weakest part of your perceived reality. So, if the weakest part is your finances, it will effect your finances. If the weakest part is relationships, it will effect your relationships. Negative energy is ultimately trying to stop you from invoking the completeness of the Law of Attraction. It wants to stop you from achieving what you desire in your life. These are genuine energies that can affect your life.

So what happens when you apply the Law of Attraction? Well, if you put the Law of Attraction to work and have absolutely no fear, doubt or apprehension and are absolutely certain, then you've become bullet-proof. However, if there is the smallest amount of doubt or fear in your mind, if there is a negative spirit or black magic being invoked, or negative thoughts involved, it will affect your attraction energy field. How many times have you experienced an exciting opportunity coming into your life but after you tell people, the whole situation falls apart? This is evidence of others judgments and thoughts carrying a negative effect on your goals. My grandmother used to say that when you're going after a goal, don't tell anyone. Keep your mouth shut. When you tell people, their natural instinct is to be jealous and critical.

At one point I really desired to move, but every time moving opportunities arose, it was like there was a giant magnet in the ground keeping me stuck. Something would always manifest to prevent me from leaving. I later found out just how many people surrounding me in my life did not want me to move. I understand now that the people around me were creating this negative magnetic energy with their thoughts.

Very few of us are bulletproof naturally. Through Miracle Mentoring and Alchemy Life Coaching, I have helped countless people change their thinking to become more and more bulletproof to negative spirits and thoughts. If you have negative spirits working on you, you must first rid yourself of them. You cannot build the empire, life and the relationship you desire if you have black magic affecting you.

If you've got negativity and darkness hampering you, this is a serious situation. Take action to clear it out. How do you clear it out? Incantations, affirmations, simple cleansing rites along with prayer are positive ways to banish negativity from your life. My favorite simple cleansing rite is to cleanse yourself and your physical environment with a lemon juice and sea salt.

Another good idea is to be in a working relationship with a spiritual mentor. A spiritual mentor is somebody who can help you find a spiritual center within yourself and your life. The fact is, having a strong spiritual core is enough to melt away most of the negativity that may be coming at you. Your spiritual core might come from Christianity, Jewish Tradition, Paganism, or New Thought beliefs.

Many find solace in the teachings of Buddha or the Hindu philosophy. I am convinced it makes little difference to the Universe which spiritual path you are on. Your spiritual core could even be a combination of many beliefs or philosophies. If you know for a fact that you are struggling on a spiritual level right now, you're questioning and wondering about why you're even here, then you are much more vulnerable to dark energy attacks.

A good mentor will help you find a spiritual core without telling you what your core is. Your spiritual guide shouldn't tell you to believe in Jesus, or keep the Sabbath Holy, or go to a certain church. A true spiritual mentor says, "Hey, who are you? Really deep down inside, what do you desire to be? What do you desire to feel about reality?" Your mentor should ask questions that guide you to draw your own conclusions about the spiritual reality that you believe within the deepest parts of yourself.

The truth is that none of us have a grip on reality. Honestly, our only knowledge of reality is what we believe it to be. **Reality is a belief system and nothing more.** So, what I'm looking for when I work with clients is establishing belief systems that empower them. For example, if you believe that these spirits can hurt you, how can that empower you? It's not a beneficial belief to entertain. So, I choose to believe that these spirits cannot hurt me in any way. If you believe that evil magic can hurt or damage you, then you are giving those negative beliefs a doorway into your subconscious mind. This mindset will likely cause the goals you have to begin falling apart because you have opened a doorway to negative energy directed at you.

Your belief system is essential when it comes to negative forces and black magic. You must find a belief system that is empowering to you. Think of it this way: You are here on Earth, but on Earth, there is no belief system that has a monopoly on anything. All the belief systems are just based on people's perceptions of reality. So, if it's based on people's perceptions of reality, why not find one that works for you and empowers you? Find one that wakes you up in the morning full of life, energy and excitement. Discover beliefs that place you in the driver's seat, place you in control of your life and guide your actions toward your goals.

Next, study that belief system until it completely fill yours thoughts and directs your action. If you are a Hindu, start memorizing parts of the Bhagavad Gita that you find empowering. If you are a Christian, begin reading the Bible and writing scriptures that banish negative thoughts on note cards to carry with you. (My personal favorite is Psalm 93.) Start surrounding yourself with people who share similar beliefs. The more you fill yourself with that energy and light, the stronger your internal spiritual core will become. This is the key to what protects you from other's negative thoughts, evil energies and dark magic.

The other skill I recommend developing is some kind of energetic clearing ritual that you can practice every day; preferably, twice a day. It might be saying the Lord's Prayer, or doing a chakra meditation. If you're Jewish, there are some wonderful daily rites using the text of the Torah. Catholics might want to learn the steps to the powerful ritual of the Breast Plate of St. Patrick. My personal preference is the Lesser Banishing Ritual of the Pentagram. (The details of this ritual can be found in Appendix B.)

The Lesser Banishing Ritual of the Pentagram is wonderful ritual that is used to eradicate negative and unwanted forces. When I say negative and unwanted forces, I am not only talking about the forces known to the conscious mind, but also those forces known to the subconscious mind. The Lesser Banishing Ritual of the Pentagram I perform is in the tradition of the Esoteric Order Golden Dawn (www.esotericgoldendawn.com), but there are other variations of this rite, too.

As you change the energy of the above world, you will see a change in the below world of Earth. If you regularly do cleansing and clearing work but still have this torturous, almost demonic energy coming into your life that is destroying your ability to manifest your goals, you need to hire a professional to get rid of the dark forces. Please do not look to psychics and palm readers as professionals. They tend to amplify the problem to insure continued business. Remember, a lack of results could mean you have counter-intentions which need be illuminated for you by an outside perspective.

One of the ways an outside perspective can illuminate that which is causing negative energy is through hypnosis and Neurolinguistic Alchemy. Trained professionals like myself know how to discover, unlock, and repair energy breaches from the inside out. Everyone has beliefs that have been hammered into their subconscious minds since birth. These beliefs are usually thought to help you in the journey of life, but at some point, they become a hindrance to your dreams.

Let me give you an example of one belief your parents might have ingrained in you that is holding you in negative energy patterns. I am sure you have heard your mother and father say, "Money doesn't grow on trees!" or, "What do you think, I'm made of money?" These words are not the ideal way to instill good spending habits and teach about creating a budget, although that is what parents want for their child. Those kinds of statements by parents act as magical attacks on children that actually stop them from reaching their earning potential as adults. This belief that no longer serves you must be repaired from the inside out. If you don't transform those beliefs, you are leaving yourself vulnerable for other people's negative thoughts, feelings and energies to work against you. No matter how much you are trying to create a positive, personal empire using the Law of Attraction, if you are still being hampered deep down in your subconscious mind by negative beliefs others instilled in you, then your mind is under negative attack. It is vital to come to an understanding that you need to get into the depths of your beliefs to clear out any black magic you are doing on yourself.

Sometimes, when I am doing hypnosis and Neurolinguistic Alchemy with a client, I discover that my client has made vows in a past life that are being carried over into this life. These vows can be vows of chastity, poverty, servitude or silence, just to name a few. Any past beliefs can act as black magic and negative energy in this life. Not all black magic is caused by witches and voodoo dolls, but certainly some of it is. The good news is that you have the power to create a spiritual defense against anyone else's negative thoughts that might be directed at you. You also have the ability to add clearing and cleansing practices into your daily routine. You can also hire a trained Miracle Mentor and Alchemy Life Coach to discover how to rewire negative beliefs, turning them into positive power. There is no negative energy, black magic, or evil that cannot be transformed into powerful Law of Attraction action.

CHAPTER 18: SYMPTOMS OF DARK ENERGY ATTACK

"If you don't know where you are going,

you'll end up someplace else."

Yogi Berra

This chapter is about expanding your arsenal of Law of Attraction understanding with information other gurus are rarely qualified to discuss. The world is full of cotton candy beliefs that lack fuel to empower your life. For many people all over the world that are being attacked by negative energy, cotton candy gurus will not empower their ability to live the life they desire. Negative energy comes in many different forms from a number of different sources. When negative energy is surrounding you, you must have a plan to break the state of negativity. This will allow you to quickly return to a positive attraction state of being. As I share the symptoms of being a victim of negative energy flow, you will become keenly aware of the patterns you must change to empower your abilities to attract the life you desire.

The Law of Attraction is a way of causing reality to conform to will so that you attract the life you desire; a life filled with love, money, health, joy and happiness. In fact, this is the definition of "magic". Magic is *the art and science of causing reality to conform to will.* Science gives the understanding of how to make attraction an art. The problem is, out of all of the Law of Attraction coaches in the world, none of them will tell you what action to take when disaster fills your life.

Here is the absolute truth. **There are negative forces flowing in the world that are focused on stopping you from attracting what you desire.** When you are not aware that negative energy is working on your life, it is easy to get wrapped up in an energy flow that will take you in the opposite direction of your goals and dreams. Sometimes, these negative forces are from mean-spirited, jealous people who hired a dark magician or dark energy practitioner to work against you. It is not hard to find a magician for hire on the internet that will focus negative energy on anyone you want. These negative forces can be so intense, so strong and so powerful that it can rip your life apart.

Some people say, "Well, my scientific objectivity will keep me from falling into this kind of negative energy because I don't really believe in it", or they say, "I go to church on a regular basis, therefore there is no room for negative energy in my life." Scientific and religious beliefs will help repel negative forces, but they are not foolproof protection. You may be one of many that have come to a point in life where everything is falling apart and you are left dumbfounded wondering why. This is because you are not equipped with the knowledge of the symptoms of negative energy. There are nine components to your life and once one starts to fall apart, all nine start to crumble. When all nine are ripped apart, life provides very little pleasure.

All forms of thought have at least two components or two sides to them. So, as much as you may be thinking positive thoughts, focused on your goals, and visualizing the goals you desire to manifest, there can easily be counter-forces invoked by other people or even your own subconscious mind attacking you. There are always belief and non-belief aspects of attraction thoughts. For example, you might feel very courageous in starting your own company, but you are afraid to ask for investors. You might be excited about building a relationship with the love of your life, but despise the thought of sharing a bed. These are example of thoughts that are counter-intentions, which are often your own worst enemy. **When your mind is filled with counter-intentions and counter-thoughts, it's as if you're doing black magic on yourself.**

You do not always need to feel the threat of a magician or a black magic practitioner to see symptoms of negative energy in your life. As stated above, it could just be your own counter-intentions. There are other times when a group of people get together and focus their attention in your direction. This can have some real negative consequences. For example, everyone in the office might talk about one person and what this individual is doing wrong. When everybody is invoking negative thoughts, it creates a type of negative magical cloud around that person. (The cloud may look like Pig Pen from the "Peanuts" cartoon by Charles M. Schulz.) In addition, people thousands of miles away who are holding negative thoughts can be hurting you, too.

What's the secret? Well, first off, you have to understand that it's all possible. I know people who have lost their business, health, family and wealth because negative thoughts were being focused on them by people in their circle of influence. When this happens, you must take action *FAST*. Many times, it's as simple as cutting these people out of your energy field. Literally, just say, **"I am pushing all negative people out of my energy field as I raise and stand in my own positive attraction energy."** Repeat this 100 times a day until you are certain that their negative thoughts are neutralized.

Who are these people that cause negative energy in your life? Sometimes they're your best friends, family, or part of your church and social community. Often, these people believe that they have your best interest at heart. They have these negative thoughts about how you are living your life and they emotionalize them as if your life was theirs. The power of having these negative thoughts comes through the continued emotionalizing and visualizing of what they believe should be happening in your life. Negative thoughts focused on you by a number of people, or even someone who is a very powerful emotional person, disturbs your energy field.

If you're a deeply spiritual person and you are trying to open yourself up to higher vibration, Divine Light and higher consciousness, don't be surprised by some kind of resistance. That's the way it works; you're rising up so there's going to be a counter-force. You can overcome this negative gravitational pull with a strong will and focus on building increased spiritual energies within your sphere of sensation. Sometimes negativity comes not from anybody specific, but through the way energy flows in the Universe to teach you valuable lessons. Sometimes you believe a situation is negative when it is not negative at all.

All of these thoughts and forces can have a powerful effect on you. The key is to learn how to identify some of the symptoms that manifest when negative magic, spells and hexes are coming against you. When you identify them, it is the first step in creating a plan to counteract or repel the negativity. Be aware that your mind will want to get into logical thinking, which is designed to talk you out of taking action against the negativity. When you tell yourself that it's just your imagination or a coincidence, you will not make any progress in removing the negativity. This is why you must learn to recognize the following symptoms of negative energy attack. Usually, one of these symptoms alone is no reason to think you are under magical attack. It is when there are multiple symptoms of negativity that you must evaluate the situation and take the proper action.

The first symptom you need to trust is that uneasy feeling. If you wake up in the morning and feel that something bad is about to happen, trust that feeling. Most people have had a bad experience happen to them who have felt it coming two or three days prior to the event. What most people failed to do is trust their instincts and take action to uncover the source of the uneasy feeling. This is often seen when a family member is about to pass on. You find yourself thinking about them when you usually don't. These are your instincts attempting to guide your actions.

You need to trust your instincts. Usually, uneasy feelings will come in the morning rather than the evening. While you are sleeping, your mind compiles all the thoughts and feelings from the day into a form of order in your dream state so you are refreshed for the new day. In the morning, there's no reason to feel shaky or uneasy unless your gut level intuition is trying to communicate a warning to you. If you have that uneasy feeling every single morning, you need to start recording and analyzing those fears. If you don't know what those fears are and you can't identify them, it's what psychologists would call free-floating anxiety. Make special note of this because free-floating anxiety is one of the major symptoms of magical or negative energy coming against you.

You're calling your friends up and they don't answer or return your calls. Next, you call your family and they don't respond either. When you notice little by little, people that were there for you are no longer there, you have identified another symptom of negativity or serious oppression. **People that were open to you who are no longer open to you is a serious sign of negativity in your energy field.**

When people start closing down toward you, sometimes it's for a legitimate reason, like maybe you didn't keep your word. However, there's a certain legitimacy that, in relationships with friends and families, there are going to be those kinds of situations but people resolve them and move on. So when people say, "I don't want to talk about it" or they just clam up or don't return your phone call or email, it is often a sign of negative energy interfering in your life and relationships.

In all truth, there's no reason why a good friend or family member just isn't there or suddenly turns against you, except as a result of negative energy. People that have it good avoid negative energy like the plague. I had a very close friend of 17 years that I talked to everyday and all of a sudden he wouldn't take my phone calls anymore. There was no reason for this. I later found out who was focusing negative intent on breaking my circle of support. It was a jealous individual focusing negative energy on me to split up the relationship. Removing this individual changed the energy and removed the issue.

The third symptom of negativity is that too many things begin to go wrong all at once. You don't just get a flat tire, you get a flat tire and the spare has gone flat. Then you get the tires fixed and the radiator pops. In other words, you are in a chain reaction of disaster. Have you been there? This can be a sign that there is focused negativity directed at you.

Losing a job or being unable to find work is the fourth symptom of negativity. Maybe you're going on interviews and you have more credentials than other candidates, but you still don't get hired. Guess what? Someone is zapping you with negative energy and you better wake up. This negativity is real and could completely destroy your foundation of home, family and friends.

When you see these first four symptoms you must take serious action by protecting yourself and invoking counter-forces. Don't talk yourself out of action by saying this negativity is just a coincidence. If you don't create an action plan for repelling the negativity, then you run the risk of your life being consumed by negativity.

The fifth symptom of negativity is that your sexual energy dies down. Sexual energy is normal in human beings, but when suddenly you have no interest, you are under attack. When you say to yourself, "It's not that I couldn't, it's just that nothing is there," you need to take action against negativity. Your energy field is being messed with; it's being manipulated, either consciously or subconsciously. Either someone is personally attempting to manipulate your energy field or through your own negative counter-thoughts, your energy field is being affected.

The sixth symptom is declining health. You are under attack if you spontaneously get a cold when it's not even cold season. An attack on your health could also appear as an overall icky feeling, weakness in your muscles, random headaches or digestive issues. If you find the symptoms of illness along with people turning away, an uneasy feeling and too many things going wrong in your life, then you have more than enough symptoms to show that negativity is hindering your ability to attract the life you desire. There is a breach in your energy field and you are no longer in control of the Law of Attraction bringing you the life and health you desire.

Beware that certain parts of the world have a higher percentage of negative energy practitioners. Have you recently traveled to Louisiana, Florida, South Africa, or the Middle East? **Travel is the seventh symptom of negativity.** In these areas, especially in the Middle East, there is an excess of negative energy magic being projected. My clients from the Middle East often fall prey to Djinn magic which is a serious form of black magic. Djinn magic takes on a unique fiery form of very powerful, sticky negative energy. Even after the practitioner has forgotten about you, this fiery negative energy lingers on. You might have had a carefree travel experience, but either the natives are trying to keep you from returning, or you unknowingly offended someone. It could be that someone felt you did not tip enough or thought you gave them a dirty look.

The eighth symptom is that you feel violated. You feel as though there is an energy out there making you feel that everyone is out to get you. It may be that your boss or coworkers are against you, or your ideas are always being declined. Sometimes the feeling of a shadow following you or a cloud overhead is an indication of negative energy. There may be energy that violates you at night; it may wake you up, rattle the doors, and make objects go "bump in the night." Often, it is natural objects that go "bump", but there are times when supernatural noises and events are very real. A negative energy surrounding you can build up so much strength that it has to have an outlet or path of release. That outlet is the physical environment around you. A good way to prevent your environment from becoming a path of release is to clear, banish and prepare your environment into a positive or neutral environment before going to bed. Clearing and neutralizing your nightly resting place is a wonderful protection practice to do when traveling. Let me give you an example of the kind of energy violation and path of release I am talking about.

I am very skeptical about anomalies, but I know how to acknowledge energy phenomenon. One night I was lying in bed, when the indoor shutters started shaking violently, to the point where I had to believe there was someone on the other side shaking them. I checked outside but there was no person, creature, or wind to give an explanation for this phenomenon. As the shutters continued going crazy., I realized that I had forgotten to banish the negative energies before bed, from an individual who was seeking to destroy me. If you are not trained to clear energy, this is the type of violation and oppression where you need to seek professional help to get rid of the negativity. I then banished the energies, commanding them to depart. The shutters stopped moving and I was able to sleep peacefully.

The ninth and last symptom is nightmares. If you're having an unreasonable amount of nightmares, it can be a sign of negative energy working its way into your subconscious mind. When this happens, it can put you into a place where you're going to feel fear, doubt and anxiety. These feelings all work against your Law of Attraction practice. Learn to take note of your dreams. Can you connect the elements of your dreams to things that are helping or hurting your attraction work? Look for ways to reverse the negative elements of nightmares into positive attraction actions.

Take a deep look at each of these nine symptoms of negative energy. How many can you see in your life? What actions can you take to reverse and counteract the symptoms you have? If you have all of these symptoms together, it means you need to **TAKE ACTION RIGHT NOW!** Even if you have half of them, there's a good chance you have a problem. Remember, thoughts attract things. As you take action to clear and cleanse yourself and your environment, you will remove the negative energy and make way for positive attraction in your life. You will see that as you start using the Law of Attraction, your dreams and desires will come into your reality.

Note: If you believe you are a victim of negative energy and need specialized help, write to me at lawofattractionsolutions@gmail.com. Either I or a qualified colleague will assist in removing the negativity.

CHAPTER 19: BEWARE! 7 SERIOUS ATTRACTION MISTAKES

"Whatever the mind of man

can conceive and believe,

it can achieve"

Napoleon Hill

We all have days when everything seems to go haywire. You know what I'm talking about; the day when you got a flat tire, then the television blew up, and you burnt dinner. It seems that anything that can go wrong, will go wrong (Murphy's Law). Interestingly, it all seems to happen in one or two days. Here is some sobering news: **However hard this may be to swallow, the Law of Attraction teaches that somehow, some way, you have attracted those bad days, as well as all the good days.** We're not exactly sure how we do it, but somehow we attract those days when everything goes haywire.

Remember, where you direct your attention, emotions, and expectation is where your attraction will happen. When you expect a dream to manifest beyond any shadow of a doubt, then you are planting a seed in the Universe, and you can expect a miracle to happen in your life. The problem is that you and I are all filled with counter-intentions, mind viruses or doubts. I am sure that you know of people that were on top of their game and had it all, then one day everything fell apart. Usually, when the stability of life is shattered, there's more involved than just that one day. You will usually find that you didn't take the extra precautions to make sure you had the files backed up in the computer, or your seat belt on, or any of the other safety precautions you could have taken. Let me share seven mistakes that you may be making when you are trying to attract your heart's desire.

No matter what you are trying to attract, there is nothing more powerful in the entire world than taking intentional action. I work with many business clients who seek help with marketing their business. When business owners call me and hire my services, it's usually because they have gone through many other advisers and done everything under the sun but are still not attracting the kind of money they desire. They are making $5,000 instead of $5 million. I can usually tell when I begin working with a client how successful we will be from the very beginning. The people who start out saying, "Well, I need time to think about it..." are the ones who don't attract the outcomes they desire. Those that create a plan in which specific steps are set in motion attract more than their wildest dreams. Those that take immediate action always see miracles. **All attraction comes with action.**

Andrew Carnegie was the richest man in the world at one time. His massive amounts of wealth came from steam lines and steel mills. He used to time his future managers with a stopwatch. He would ask them a question but if it took them any longer than 30 seconds to decide what they wanted to do, then he wouldn't hire them for the job. The reason he wouldn't hire them is because he felt that successful people already knew what they desired, so that when opportunity arose, action was taken quickly and decisively.

When you know what your goals are, you do not have to take time to question whether an action is in line with your goals. Successful people just know. They say, "I am saving this relationship," or "I am paying off my debt," and they don't need time to think it over. **Successful people know what they desire and never lose sight of that vision.** They can make up their mind in 30 seconds because they know when opportunities meet their vision. They know it's important and they know what they need to do.

According to Carnegie, unsuccessful people make up their mind slowly and change their mind quickly. They don't really know what they want to do. **Unsuccessful people don't have a vision, they don't have a purpose and they don't have a destination.** Out of all the common Law of Attraction mistakes I will share below, nothing is more destructive than having goals that are not well-defined.

Mistake 1: Believing that positive thinking is enough to attract what you want. There are people who walk around and preach positive thinking as if they read it out of the Bible. Positive thinking is great but it's not always possible to think positive. There will be times in life when something changes your inner thought process and if your success depends on your ability to think positively 24 hours a day, then you are in trouble. There is more to manifesting what you desire than just positive thinking. Positive thinking is important, but it's not the end all-be all.

Mistake 2: Becoming impatient. It is easy to put out an

intention to the Universe. It is easy to get excited and have a sense of expectation when you get up the next morning. It is also just as easy to become impatient. No matter how strongly you create a vision of owning a new car, today and maybe for the next few days, you're still riding the bus. No matter how great the vision and intention of a car is, parts of your mind will still feel like walking onto the bus is like cold water being thrown on your face. The simple action of getting on the bus tells you that you still don't have that car. At this point it is extremely easy to become impatient and angry at the thought that you do not have a car. Once you get impatient you will dry up the excited attraction energy that was flowing just moments earlier. The point is, when you become impatient, you are destroying your path to attract your dreams. You are hurting your opportunity to allow energy to flow into your reality.

Mistake 3: Playing the guessing game. Spending time trying to guess what the Universe is going to do will limit your outcome. In trying to determine ahead of time how and when you will attract what you desire, you can miss the unexpected ways your dreams can be fulfilled. In other words, you are limiting the Universe. The Universe has an infinite amount of materials it can use to manifest what you can't manifest for yourself. Don't limit the Universe. If you desire a new car, a new home, or a dream vacation, don't limit the Universe! Let the Universe bring unique opportunities to your door. You might win a car in a game show or be a top seller winning a dream vacation. You might get a raise or get informed that a bunch of money you never expected has been left in your name. It is very important to give the Universe the freedom to work so that the outcome will arrive quickly.

Mistake 4: Allowing your emotions to be led by external evidence. Although every piece of evidence in your life may point out that you are "losing" or "it's not going to work", you must never allow your emotions to believe the idea of not achieving your attraction goals. Expect to have miracles happen in your life! The external evidence means nothing. Energy is always changing and flowing. I have seen couples who split up, move out and put restraining orders on each other come back together to build a beautiful new relationship by invoking the Law of Attraction. I don't care what the external evidence is, you are going to have the life that you desire, but you have to believe in the Law of Attraction and in unlimited possibilities. You must stop sabotaging yourself through emotional weakness and take some hard-core, concrete action. Action and especially emotionalizing what you desire, no matter how the circumstances may appear, is absolutely essential: without that, there's no guarantee of anything.

Mistake 5: Holding on to limiting beliefs. This is a game changer when mastered. People have so many limiting beliefs. Have you ever said anything like, "I'm too old; I'm too young; I'm too dumb; I don't have a degree; I'm too small; I'm too big; I'm not friendly enough, or I don't have the right life experiences?" Take an honest look at yourself. You have the ability to manifest everything you desire. It starts with believing in yourself. If there is any goal that is important to you, then you must be willing to throw yourself on the fire of transformation to change limiting beliefs into unlimited beliefs.

Mistake 6: Not clearing your energy field and thinking. There are so many people that are carrying around heavy negative energy from the past, present, and worries of the future. One of the shifts I often activate in a person's life through Miracle Mentoring and Alchemy Life Coaching is to change his or her thinking. A transformation of a client's thinking allows the negative energy to be cleared from their mind. An unclear mind and foggy energy field is filled with many counter-intentions. Counter-intentions are holding you back from having an extraordinary life. You are just as smart as any person out there. You must believe it. What do you desire? Do you desire to have an increased income, get a promotion or work for a new company? You might think, "I don't have the skills I need to work for a new company." This is unclear thinking. Thoughts like this reveal a limiting belief pattern which creeps into your future success, then chokes off the manifestation of your goals.

Do this right now. Write down five limiting beliefs, then take that piece of paper and throw it in a fire. Burn it up and say these words five times, "Never again." Also say, "Never again will I stoop down to allow unclear limiting beliefs about my life and myself stop my dreams. Never again." Limiting beliefs are horrid, so getting clear is absolutely essential. The Law of Attraction is working all the time; it can either be working for you or against you.

Mistake 7: Failing to take action. You need to take action while it's hot; while it's on your mind and part of your reality. DO IT NOW! Sit down and make a list, consult a partner, draw up a plan. Take some kind of power action right now. That action will set in motion a whole slew of opportunity-creating energy. All kinds of favorable circumstances manifest when you take action. **The most common reason for a missed opportunity is a failure to take action.** Dreams only become reality with action. Don't be one of

189

those people that procrastinates. **DO IT NOW!**

This is your life we're talking about. This is your time on Earth we're talking about; this is your family, your health, your wealth. You don't have to be a slave of negativity or anything else. You can have what you desire in this life. I firmly believe that. It only takes some determined action to get the energy flowing. Others may doubt you and say, "You better not travel that road," but if that's where your heart's desire is, then get on the road right now by taking action!

Take a careful look at these common Law of Attraction mistakes. Using a notebook, analyze the evidence of each mistake within yourself. Write down how you will change yourself to eliminate the thoughts and behavior that is causing you to fall into these mistakes.

Go confidently in the direction of your dreams and throw yourself into your goals. Be determined that your positive, emotionalized dreams are becoming a reality. You are going to win. Congratulations!

CHAPTER 20: YOUR HESITATION IS KILLING YOUR DREAMS

"You are in the perfect position

to get there from here."

Abraham-Hicks

Many of you have seen the movie or read the book called "The Secret." The movie is based on the Law of Attraction as taught by Hermes, author of an ancient document called "The Emerald Tablet". If you haven't experienced "The Secret", it is a good overview to start understanding the Law of Attraction. While it is an amazing, inspirational movie, it is a meta-movie. It talks about broad ideas, but it doesn't get into specifics of attraction. Throughout this chapter and all the previous chapters, I imparted to you specific attraction secrets not found in any other book on the subject. The secrets are from years of studying the ancient mysteries, neurolinguistics, hypnosis, success cultures, business and abundance leaders. The knowledge of the secrets I share reach well beyond my studies and into many years of personal mentoring experiences.

I have had the incredible pleasure of mentoring so many different people from all over the world. This has brought me wonderful learning experiences and has broadened my horizons. Clients from Australia, Romania, India, Europe, Russia, Africa and

South America have helped me to understand the details of human nature and behaviors in every culture. Every experience I have with a client better prepares me to help other clients and you.

I also have years of energy work training. I am Imperator General of the Esoteric Order of the Golden Dawn, which is a magical group that teaches energy movement through ritual. I am also Founding Grand Master of the Ruach Healing Method. Though I find that the Ruach Healing Method is a more powerful energy healing system, there are still many times when my 18th degree Grand Master Reiki training is what I employ. Energy work is intensely influential. The more you understand energy, the more creative power you have. This is because the Universe, with all your dreams and hopes, is created from energy. It's all energy; there are just different layers of it.

So my mission, when I work with a client, is to uncover what the client really desires in life. Then, I help people just like you take action by using ancient secrets, the Magic of Light and modern mind technologies. This knowledge is what makes Miracle Mentoring and Alchemy Life Coaching unbelievably successful. In all the mentoring that I have done and will continue to do, there is one challenge that I run into again, and again, and again. This problem may be the most important secret in this whole book. Here it is: **YOUR HESITATION IS KILLING YOUR DREAMS!**

There are some people out there right now who have been thinking about getting into a new business for the last 5, 10 or 20 years. I have a friend who dreams of opening up a healing herb shop with massage therapists and hypnotherapists. However, all she's done is talk about it for the last TEN YEARS! She hungers for it to become a reality, but then she comes up with twenty reasons why she can't **DO IT NOW.** She has yet to even write a list of herbs she plans to stock. Her hesitation in taking action is killing her dreams. She is not truly inspired by her dream.

Your extraordinary life is founded in the word *inspiration.* Inspiration comes from the Greek word that means "In spirit." When you are inspired, you are filled with life; you are filled with ideas; you are full of motivation, and you have all the kinds of energy that is required to make miracles manifest.

Some people lose their inspiration in their 30's. They get a job, buy a truck, buy a fishing pole and that's that. Other people never lose their inspiration. Every town has people that are on fire in their 60's, 70's, 80's and even into their 90's. These people don't think, "I'm too old" or "I don't have enough money." These people think, "Every obstacle can be overcome, even if I have to ask ten thousand people about it before I find the answer." **Successful people simply don't live with the fear of failure as a shadow following them around.** They are excited about life and treat it as an adventure. In their mind, every dream is already a reality in another plane of existence. All they have to do is take action until their dreams catch up on the physical plane. **Successful people know there is no room for hesitation.** There is no time in the physical plane to waste hesitating to act on fulfilling your dreams.

One person who is an example of this is the late fitness guru, Jack LaLanne. As a kid, I remember watching this guy on television doing all these exercises and I thought, "Wow! Look at the muscles on this man!" Years later, he was still on television at 92, 94, and even 96 years old doing commercials! He was so inspired that he was still swimming miles each day and lifting weights in his 90's. Jack LaLanne lived to be 96 years old, and there is one important key. The key is that he didn't live in a bed until he was 96. He was fully alive, energetic and still in the game! He was active and doing everything just like he did when he was in his 30's. He still had incredible muscle tone. Jack LaLanne worked out every day because he was inspired. He was "in the spirit." He never hesitated on his dreams. **Every day was about taking action toward bigger dreams and goals.**

I don't know what your religious beliefs are but I want you to write this down: **"Nothing is impossible with God because with God, all things are possible."** I know that everyone can have a different description or definition of God. So, feel free to connect with whatever you believe God to be. God may be The Invisible One, The Creative One, Universal Energy, Buddha, Brahman, Mother Nature, or called by another name. Whatever you believe God to be, it is through your connection with God that you become fully inspired. Inspired is when you are in the Spirit and the Spirit is working through you. **In the Spirit, you are alive and energetic.**

It is easy to be motivated after a deep spiritual experience. You feel the fire and passion of being "In Spirit". Life experiences seem to crowd out these spiritual experiences so that, where there was once inspiration, there is now hesitation. There are many things that will cause hesitation to kill your inspiration and dreams.

The first and the most important emotion that will cause hesitation and kill your inspiration is *fear*. Fear, in most areas of our life, is a wasted emotion. If a bear is chasing you through the woods, fear is a good emotion. In that case, fear causes your heart to pump faster and blood pressure to rise so you're ready to run. On the other hand, how does fear causing sweaty palms help you in a job interview? Sweaty palms just give you a clammy, bad-impression handshake. A high percentage of the time, the fear causing sweaty palms is just an unnecessary way the mind comes up with reasons to hesitate taking action in the direction of your dreams.

When you find that fear is making you hesitate on your dreams, remember this acronym: **FEAR** is **F**alse **E**vidence **A**ppearing **R**eal. The mind can come up with all kinds of false evidence. If you are having relationship issues, the mind might say something like, "You're never going to get him back because he wasn't the right man for you," or "You're just not in her class." I have people call me all the time who desire to save their relationship, but they find more ways to hesitate than to take action. Sadly, people put off taking action, thinking that in the morning everything will have magically changed. Believing in fairies with magic wands does not replace the power of taking action. I seldom get a call two days after someone walks out of a relationship; I get the call six or nine months after the lover has left. Why let fear cause hesitation in creating a new and better relationship with the one you love? I have a client right now who is manifesting the return of her husband after three years of separation. That's a long time to wait to give me a call and begin taking action! The first ten minutes of this type of call is about all the fear-thoughts that caused hesitation to kill the dream of love. Hesitation is killing your life! **You must take action now, no matter what your fears are telling you.** Fear will hold you back! He who hesitates is often lost in fear. Fear is the glue that sticks us down and doesn't allow us to fly. It doesn't allow us to get up and move.

The next factor that will cause you to hesitate is family. During the early days of my ancient mystery and occult studies, I ran across the statement, *"Family is public enemy number one."* This has always stuck with me. Now, I don't know if family is enemy number one, but all my experience shows it to be in the top five. It's not present family dynamics, it's family experiences from 20 years ago that are holding you back from taking risks and accomplishing incredible wonders with your life. It is remembering all those idioms and axioms your family has pounded into your brain throughout generations that are causing you to hesitate.

Oftentimes, we're replaying those audio bites that we heard from our parents and grandparents. All of those tapes are playing over and over again in our mind. When something like, "life is hard work" has been heard a thousand times a year for twenty generations it becomes an absolute truth to the subconscious mind. So, you begin to believe that hard work is the only way to reach success.

Understand that your parents have not lied to you about reality rather, they have just taught you what they believe reality to be. Parents teach children what worked for *them*. In this fashion of passing down information, family is often a very powerful enemy to your personal success. Many of the thoughts that run through your head as

196

an adult were planted there while you were a child. **It is these repetitious thoughts from the past that are stuck in the subconscious mind which causes hesitation in the present moment.**

For example, you probably have heard, "Finish everything on your plate, because there are children starving in China!" The result is a society of overweight people finishing everything on their plate. These people are not even consciously aware that they are thinking about finishing their plate. It is the family thought on finishing meals that has been programmed into the subconscious mind. It is a type of hesitation that is stopping you from maintaining a healthy diet.

I recognized similar programming in my life. I made a vow to myself not to pass on that family belief. My children have developed into beautiful fit men & women. None of them have an ounce of fat. I taught them from a young age that when they were full there was no benefit in finishing everything on their plate. I told them it was okay to wrap up extra food and save it for later, when they were truly hungry. There wasn't a rule that said they had to finish everything on their plate. When my Italian grandma was with us for a meal, Grandma would be enemy number one. (I love her and miss her daily. She personally was not an enemy, but rather, it was her beliefs.) She would be in the background acting like not finishing your plate was a sin that would send you to Hell. However, I knew back then if I made the kids finish everything, they would always want to finish everything. No one needs to feel guilty for not wanting to finish everything on his or her plate.

The other part of family causing you to hesitate in the

manifestation of your dreams is the need for approval. Say you're getting ready to make an investment or start a business or you have a new relationship and you're worried to tell your family about it. In your mind, you play out what you expect to hear from each family member. You might hear: "Don't invest in that. You will lose everything," or "Why would you get into that business? You won't make a penny" or "You can't have a relationship with her. She's from the wrong side of the tracks!" or "He's too young and doesn't make enough money." After having spent the first eighteen years with your parents, it is very easy for the mind to project non-support.

Don't let parental programming cause you to hesitate taking action on your dreams. Simply understand parental thinking. Parents love you and mean well with their intentions, which are designed to protect you from harm. If you want to be your own person living an individual life, you must make your own choices without hesitation. Even if, on the surface, you release any negative input from family, parental programming can easily find residence in your subconscious mind. When it comes to the opinions of friends and family, family opinions enter the mind quickly because there is always that idea in your mind that family cares about you the most and wants the best for you. There are times when family operates out of jealousy. They don't want you to change too much or be too successful because then they wouldn't know you. Don't let any aspect of family cause you to hesitate on the opportunities that will make your dreams a reality.

Some people find that hesitation is nothing more than a habit. In other words, you become accustomed to hesitation because this behavior seems like the natural action to take. There are times when hesitation, as in taking it slowly, makes sense. However, most of the time, you will find that you over-hesitate. Could you imagine if Alexander Graham Bell had hesitated? He would have lost many patents for his inventions. In one case, Alexander beat his rival to the patent office by only hours. **You don't have the luxury to hesitate.** You need to move forward in the direction of your dreams and create miracles in your life that are incredible beyond your belief. You will move forward by applying the Law of Cause and Effect as well as the Law of Attraction.

The Law of Cause and Effect is very simple. It states: For every action there is a reaction. In other words, if you take an action, energy is going to shift the situation. Something is going to happen either way, but you have more control over the outcome by taking the action rather than by hesitating. Doing nothing just allows the forces of life to just push you around; the winds to pound you and the to waves hit you. You're just a leaf in the wind when you hesitate. **When you take no action, you have no control of your direction.**

Everyone knows that you can't control *everything*. There are just some situations out of your control. One truth is certain; you can't control *anything* when you hesitate. Why not find the situations that you can control and the situations you can affect through taking action? Anytime you feel like there is something you want or something you desire to attract, you have to take action immediately! It doesn't have to be huge action, but you have to take some action. You can get a notebook and begin writing out a plan or creating affirmations that will empower your goals. Take some kind of daily action! You can call a friend that will be excited with you or write a letter to me. It doesn't make any difference what you do so long as you don't hesitate. Show the Universe you are serious about your dreams. Don't let hesitation kill your inspiration. Be in the spirit and let the attraction action flow.

Admit to yourself that your hesitations are killing your dreams. Then, write the following words of admission down. Better yet, go have them tattooed on the palm of your hand, "DO IT NOW!" (Maybe not literally tattooed, but you get the idea.) These are the famous three words of W. Clement Stone who built a massive empire called "Combined Insurance Agency". He started with a $2,000 investment and built it into a multi-billion dollar company. He also was the founder of Success Magazine. His success came from his "do it now" attitude. In fact, he had these three powerful words -- "DO IT NOW" -- nicely engraved on the front of his desk. If the idea was worth thinking about, why not do it now? Do it before you talk to your parents about it. Do it before you think about it too much. Do it before you allow those fears to enter your mind and choke off your inspiration. Begin to leverage your desires and the dream you desire to create through action. **Action is the ultimate lever.** If you want to leverage those desires into action, do it now. Don't wait.

I will leave you with a very important technique for overcoming hesitation and taking actions to start creating the reality you desire. Pull out a piece of paper and a red pen. In red ink, write down what the pain will be if you don't take action. For example, if you're not exercising every day, what is the pain of not doing it? What is the outcome? The pain will be growing fatter and more out of shape every day, having so many health problems that you are hospitalized with thirty different tubes keeping you alive. Make the pain nasty and extreme. Focus on the pain and write it all down! "This is the pain for not exercising!"

Next, tape up this pain list where you can see it every day. This is the pain for not sticking to your exercise program. This is the pain of hesitating. This is what it will cost you in your life if you don't take action. You don't have to go to the mall and spend a couple hundred dollars on exercise clothes and equipment, that's not the real action. Remember those three words: DO IT NOW! NOW, get going on that exercise program.

The point of writing down the pain is that, when you're focused on the pain of not exercising, that pain becomes bigger than any hesitation you have. Look at the pain of not taking action on any goal you might have. When *not* taking action is more painful than taking action, you will stop hesitating on your dreams. You have to think, "Oh my god, this horrible thing will happen when I *don't* TAKE ACTION NOW!" That's a very powerful motivator for you to get into the state of action. You get into the action stage when you're in the spirit or inspired. So, focus on the pain of NOT doing it and take some inspired action.

The same principles are used to create a wonderful loving relationship. Focus on the pain of what happens if you don't take action to save the relationship. What really happens? What is the outcome? What kind of pain will I really put myself under? Look for the action steps that you can take. Get rid of the hesitation.

You can meditate until you're blue in the face and say mantras until you bleed out of your ears, but if you continue to hesitate on taking action, nothing will happen. I know you can become successful with that new business or whatever goal you are trying to accomplish. Stop allowing fear or family or anything else to cause you to hesitate and kill your dreams.

DO IT NOW!

Appendix A: The Emerald Tablet of Hermes

The following is the text of "The Emerald Tablet of Hermes", as translated by Sir Isscac Newton. This translation by Isaac Newton is found among his alchemical papers that are currently housed in King's College Library, Cambridge University.

Tis true without lying, certain & most true.

That which is below is like that which is above & that which is above is like that which is below to do the miracles of one only thing

And as all things have been & arose from one by the mediation of one: so all things have their birth from this one thing by adaptation.

The Sun is its father, the moon its mother, the wind hath carried it in its belly, the earth is its nurse.

The father of all perfection in the whole world is here.

Its force or power is entire if it be converted into earth.

Separate thou the earth from the fire, the subtle from the gross sweetly with great industry.

It ascends from the earth to the heaven & again it descends to the earth & receives the force of things superior & inferior.

By this means you shall have the glory of the whole world

& thereby all obscurity shall fly from you.

*Its force is above all force. For it vanquishes every subtle thing &
penetrates every solid thing.*

So was the world created.

*From this are & do come admirable adaptations whereof the means
(or process) is here in this. Hence I am called Hermes Trismegistus,
having the three parts of the philosophy of the whole world*

*That which I have said of the operation of the Sun is accomplished &
ended.*

Source: Isaac Newton. "Keynes MS. 28". The Chymistry of Isaac
Newton. Ed. William R. Newman June 2010. Retrieved March 4, 2013

APPENDIX B: POWER QUOTES

This list of Power Quotes has been created from the bold statements throughout this book. These statement have been transformed for use as affirmations or incantations. Use these power quotes to enhance your ability to attract your goals and to keep your mind focused on your dreams. You might select one or two from the list to use as daily affirmations. You can also read the list everyday to energize your entire being and set your mind on attracting the life of your dreams.

I am not on a journey of self-discovery; I am on a journey of self-creation.

∞

I am the unified field.

∞

I'm not just attracting a path, I AM the path. I become the path, I become the way, and I become what I AM.

∞

Freedom is all in my mind.

∞

If I control my thoughts, I will automatically control my emotions.

∞

I visualize and emotionalize my goals.

∞

I take action now.

∞

Action shows the Universe that I am serious about my goals, so everything can align to make my goals a reality.

∞

I am learning the art of manifestation through specialized knowledge.

∞

I work the matrix.

∞

I love.

∞

I control my thoughts; I control my mind.

∞

I love myself.

∞

My dominating thoughts attract the kinds of experiences I have in my life.

∞

Miracles happen when my brain, body, mind and spirit all start working in harmony with the Universe to attract the life I desire.

∞

I write it down!

∞

Everything is available to me.

∞

I actually operated as if I was already there. I operate as if the outcome has already been achieved. I talked as if it is a done deal.

∞

I take action even when I do not have the funds for the outcome I seek because I never know how the Universe will provide me with the outcome of my goals.

∞

I don't think OF my goals, I think FROM my goals.

∞

I give my goals details.

∞

I remove my counter-intentions.

∞

It isn't a matter of just thinking some way; it's a matter of taking action based on my thinking.

∞

I guard my language and use the word manifesting instead of want.

∞

Like attracts like, money attracts money, and being a loving person attracts loving relationships.

∞

I write manifesting statements.

∞

I have accountability.

∞

I shift my focus from what I don't like to what I DO like.

∞

I get clear about what I desire!

∞

As above, so below!

∞

My wish is my command.

∞

The most important time I have for building, attracting and getting what I desire is RIGHT NOW.

∞

I am that I am.

∞

The key to the "I AM" incantation is immediate action.

∞

My subconscious mind is my connecting link with the Infinite.

∞

Attraction doesn't work without action.

∞

I know how to create myself into a container for anything I desire to attract.

∞

I let Divine Source, God, the Universe, Mother Nature or whomever/whatever I call upon, take over and manifest my miracles for me!

∞

I am nature's greatest miracle.

∞

Nobody ever regrets loving.

∞

Love is the ultimate magic in the Universe.

∞

I deserve love because I am willing to give love in return. I am willing to pour my heart, soul, spirit and actions into another person.

∞

I deserve an incredible amount of love in my life. I deserve to be loved beyond anything I've ever felt or experienced. I am open to being loved all the time, 24/7.

∞

Without love there is no magic. I am full of love and see magic.

∞

It's easy to manifest love into my reality.

∞

I make love my first and last priority.

∞

True love is always becoming more powerful.

∞

I can create an extraordinary relationship.

∞

I am simply what I choose to create.

∞

The invisible connection in the universe will provide the conduit for the change.

∞

My creative visualizations will change my love life exponentially so practice creative visualization often.

∞

I understand that fear will destroy my relationship faster than anything else.

∞

I remove self-sabotaging thoughts or fears and anxieties that live within my subconscious mind.

∞

There is absolutely nothing worse than self-sabotage.

∞

When I believe something different, I attract something different.

∞

I believe the number one quality that must be within the sacred circle of my relationships is an undeniable, unstoppable trust.

∞

Lying is a counter-intention.

∞

On my last day when I'm about to take my last gasp of air, I'm not going to wish I had spent more time at the office or golf course, but I will regret not spending more time with the people I love, so I love fully daily.

∞

Whatever energies I throw into my circle of love is what the Universe will give me more of because likes attract likes.

∞

When I make a conscious effort to enhance my love, I will see the Law of Attraction and the Universe are working with me.

∞

The Law of Attraction responds to how I am vibrating and brings me more of the same.

∞

The keyword is "believe".

∞

I believe I can create an incredible circle of love that only my lover and I can ever enter; it can never be breached.

∞

I command my unconscious mind to transform me into a calm, confident, relaxed and strong individual.

∞

What I see, feel and believe I will attract.

∞

There is nothing more powerful on this Earth than two people in love who share a dream.

∞

I make my soul mate connection the dominating thought in my mind. This is the secret to attracting the love I desire.

∞

Love is a verb. Being a soul mate is an action job.

∞

I don't try, I do.

∞

Without new knowledge creating new ways to approach life, I keep getting the same results.

∞

All energy healing is directly responsive to the Law of Attraction.

∞

If I don't believe it can happen, if I come up with excuses, then forget it. It is not going to happen.

∞

What I am working to eliminate is continuous mental and physical pain. No one needs to live like that.

∞

The Law of Attraction is always at work, either for me or against me. It's my choice.

∞

When I create a vision on the higher plane of reality, it must manifest into my life.

∞

I have the power to attract incredible, unbelievable health. I have the power to attract incredible, unbelievable wealth, happiness, love or anything else I desire according to the Emerald Tablet of Hermes.

∞

I can do this.

∞

I know that I am supposed to be doing something special with my life.

∞

Once the blocks are gone the money flows, the love grows and the quality of life elevates.

∞

Hypnosis is just a relaxed state of focused concentration. Miracles happen when hypnosis is done using the Law of Attraction.

∞

Creative visualization is a powerful tool used to direct the subconscious mind like hypnosis.

∞

The clearer I visualize my goals, dreams and outcomes, the greater chance I have in gaining the inner knowledge and insight that leads me to manifest all that I desire.

∞

Forgiveness involves forgetting, letting it go and moving on.

∞

Magic is nothing more than the art and science of causing reality to conform to will.

∞

Being filled with negative energy hinders me and attracts exactly what I don't desire.

∞

I will always attract exactly what I visualize.

∞

I understand that the attitude of "want" implies a state of lack.

∞

I relax and let the Universe do the work for me.

∞

No matter what my goal, I must be willing to let it go.

∞

What I create in my mind will eventually manifest in reality.

∞

Thoughts and goals receive animation through my emotions.

∞

After inflaming my intention with visualization, passion, and certainty, I turn it over to Uriel.

∞

I don't even need to believe in angels for them to be effective in helping me manifest my desires. Nobody knows for sure what angel energy is or how it works, or if it has wings, but it is a fact that the Universe seems to act as if they are real.

∞

Angels find their purpose in fulfilling the intent of Divine Source.

∞

He is in me and I am in him.

∞

The Universe is in me.

∞

I remember that thoughts are things. .

∞

Counter-intentions are the thoughts in me mind that act like black magic on my dreams.

∞

I are bullet proof.

∞

Reality is a belief system and nothing more.

∞

When my mind is filled with counter-intentions and counter-thoughts, it's as if I am doing black magic on myself.

∞

I am pushing all negative people out of my energy field as I raise and stand in my own positive attraction energy.

∞

I trust my gut feelings.

∞

People that were open to me who are no longer open to me is a serious sign of negativity in my energy field.

∞

Symptoms of negativity include too many things going wrong all at once, losing a job or being unable to find work, sexual energy diminishing, declining health, nightmares, and traveling.

∞

I TAKE ACTION RIGHT NOW!

∞

However hard this may be to swallow, the Law of Attraction teaches that somehow, some way, I have attracted those bad days, as well as all the good days.

∞

Where I direct my attention, emotions, and expectation is where my attraction will happen.

∞

No matter what I am trying to attract, there is nothing more powerful in the entire world than taking intentional action.

∞

All attraction comes with action.

∞

I am a successful person who knows what I desire and never loses sight of that vision.

∞

Unsuccessful people don't have a vision, they don't have a purpose and they don't have a destination.

∞

Attraction mistakes that are hindering my dreams from manifesting can include, believing that positive thinking is enough to attract what I desire, becoming impatient, playing the guessing game, allowing my emotions to be led by external evidence, holding on to limiting beliefs, not clearing my energy field and thinking, and failing to take action.

∞

I do this right now.

∞

The most common reason for a missed opportunity is a failure to take action. Dreams only become reality with action. I never procrastinate. I DO IT NOW!

∞

Successful people simply don't live with the fear of failure as a shadow following them around. I am fearless & successful.

∞

I know there is no room for hesitation.

∞

Every day is about taking action toward bigger dreams and goals.

∞

Nothing is impossible with God because with God, all things are possible.

∞

In the Spirit, I am alive and energetic.

∞

FEAR is False Evidence Appearing Real.

∞

I take action now, no matter what my fears are telling me.

∞

It is these repetitious thoughts from the past that are stuck in the subconscious mind which causes hesitation in the present moment.

∞

I don't have the luxury to hesitate.

∞

When I take no action, I have no control of my direction.

∞

I admit to myself that my hesitations are killing my dreams.

∞

Action is the ultimate lever.

∞

I DO IT NOW! MY HESITATION IS KILLING MY DREAMS! I DO IT NOW!

APPENDIX C: THE LESSER BANISHING RITUAL OF THE PENTAGRAM

The Lesser Banishing Ritual of the Pentagram protection ritual begins by first calming your interior self and relaxing your whole body. You always want to be sure you are calm so that you are protecting and not trapping anxieties and fear in your sphere of sensation. Calming yourself is easily achieved by performing the Four Fold Breath.

Breathing has a vital role in connecting you to the powers of the Universe that are everywhere at all times. Calming the breath is the first step in making the connection with the Universe, Source, God, or your preferred higher power. When your breath is calm and flowing your energy is also calm and flowing. The breath exercise called the Four Fold Breath creates a clean environment for the Law of Attraction to be channeled through.

The Four Fold Breath will help you prepare for attraction work. Learning to control one's breathing in a deep, regular, harmonic rhythm helps to increase and energize the sphere of sensation of the body. This exercise is a powerful tool for increasing the amount of healthy attraction energy flowing through you. It will also put you in a higher and deeper state of mental consciousness. Learning to control your breathing is the foundation to learning to focus thoughts as you manifest with the Law of Attraction. Practice this exercise once a day to reap the most benefits. Start with maybe 4-5 minutes and slowly increase your time doing the Four Fold Breath to 15-20 minutes. You will be amazed at how good your body begins to feel within a few short days. You will also be empowered by the focus and clarity in your Law of Attraction work.

Exercise : The Four Fold Breath

"Breath is evidence of Life." – Golden Dawn Neophyte Initiation

Step 1:

Empty the lungs and remain thus while counting to four.

Step 2:

Inhale, counting to four, so that you feel filled with breath from the bottom of your lungs up to your neck or throat area.

Step 3:

Hold this breath while counting to four.

Step 4:

Exhale counting to four until your lungs are empty.

This should be practiced counting slowly and quietly until you find a rhythm that suits you and helps you feel comfortable and still. Having attained this, count the breath for 2-3 minutes or until you are completely quieted and relaxed. You may then proceed with a the Lesser Banishing Ritual of the Pentagram to clear your space. This clearing ritual begins with a prayer called "The Kabbalistic Cross".

The Kabbalistic Cross is a beautiful way to begin and end all of your "Ritual and Clearing Work." It is prayer that brings down the Light of Divine Source vertically and extends the Light horizontally.

Exercise: The Kabbalistic Cross Prayer

"Ateh Malkuth

Ve-Geburah, Ve-Gedulah,

Le-olam

Amen"

Step 1:

Stretch both of your arms straight out to your sides into the form of a cross. Visualize a glowing white light about your head. Take your right hand and gently plunge your index finger into that light which is above your head and will it to be drawn down as you touch your forehead. Have it rest upon your forehead as you vibrate, **"Ateh"**, pronounced *Ah-TAH*. This should be pronounced elongated. This means: **FOR THINES IS...**

Step 2:

Bring the point of your finger firmly down your body while willing the light on your forehead to follow along as you point toward the ground at your feet. Visualize the light now covering your feet and vibrate, **"Malkuth"**, pronounced *Mahl-KOOT*. This means: **THE KINGDOM...**

Step 3:

Now bring your finger up to your right shoulder, touching it gently. As you do this, visualize the sphere of white light running up through the center of your body, forming a beam of light into your heart area shooting out to your right side to the end of your right hand. Focus on this beam and vibrate, **"Ve-Geburah"**, pronounced *Vih-Gi-Boo-RAH*. This means: **THE POWER...**

Step 4:

Move your finger and the sphere of light to your left shoulder, touch it gently. Visualize all through this process another beam of light connecting from your heart area ending at the tip of your finger on your left hand. Vibrate, **"Ve-Gedulah"** pronounced *Vih-Gi-Doo-LAH*. This means: **AND THE GLORY...**

Step 5:

Clasp your hands together at your chest in a praying stance while visualizing within you a cross made of light that covers your entire body. Vibrate, **"Le-olam"**, pronounced *Lay-Oh-LAHM*. This means: **FOREVER & EVER...**

Step 6:

End by vibrating **"Amen"**, pronounced *AH-men*. This means: **SO BE IT**.

The word "Amen" in Hebrew translates into "so be it." Amen is a notarikon. A notarikon is made by taking the first letter of each word of a sentence and forming a new word. Amen is taken from the phrase: El Melech Neheman, which means "God is our faithful King." This is the mystical meaning behind the word "Amen".

With all of these words put together it forms the prayer: **"For Thine is the kingdom and the power and the glory forever. Amen."** Does this sound familiar? It should! For it is derived from one of the oldest prayers in the Bible. You will find this same phrase found near the end of the Lord's Prayer.

Exercise: The Lesser Banishing Ritual of the Pentagram

The Lesser Banishing Ritual of the Pentagram, (L.B.R.P.), is a simple protection exercise that can be memorized quickly. Some say it only takes an hour to memorize. Applying the L.B.R.P. to your Law of Attraction work is a powerful tool for transforming energy. When you are about to clear old or negative energy from yourself or space be sure that you invoke the power and the presence of the Divine Source to guide you and protect you. This applies when you are using the Lesser Banishing Ritual of the Pentagram or any other method of your choice. The advantage of L.B.R.P. is that the ritual invokes of the power of the Archangels. Archangels protect you from doubt and others' options. As you practice and learn the L.B.R.P., you will experience the power of this ritual.

First, start by performing the Kabbalistic Cross which is above.

Step 1:

Stand in the East and face East. Draw a pentagram in a brilliant flaming blue. Draw it in front of you, at the distance of one full arm's length. Using your right hand begin at your left hip. See the line being drawn and following the line up to the apex of the pentagram at the level of your head, down to your right hip, then across your body to the

Illustration 1: Pentagram of the L.B.R.P.

222

furthest left of your body at the level of your shoulders, across your body again to the furthest right of your body at the level of your shoulders, and completing the pentagram by ending it where you first began at your left hip.

Step 2 :

Inhale through the nose. As you do, drawn into you the sphere of light above your head and let it mend with your breath. Feel the energy coursing and rushing through your lungs and body. Step forward with the left foot. At the same time, lift up both arms above your head, then bring your hands down to ear-

Illustration 2: Sign of the Enterer

height, palms facing in, and thrust both of your hands forward with all fingers extended outward with index fingers almost coming together as

Illustration 3:
Sign of Silence

a point, palms facing the ground, pointing at the exact middle of the glowing blue pentagram in front of you. This is the Sign of the Enterer. As you do this, vibrate YHVH: "Yod Heh Vav Heh".

Remember, when vibrating be sure to elongate each word in a continuous flow, using one full breath. As you vibrate this vocally, mentally hear the name echo throughout the eastern ends of the Universe. The same will go for the South, West and North. Revert your left foot back. Now place the point of your left index finger to your lips, in the form of silence. This is the form of Harpocrates, the Sign of Silence.

Step 3:

Once again, point at the center of the pentagram that you have just drawn, using the index finger of your right hand. Trace a brilliant white line from the center of the pentagram and follow it to the South. This will form an arc of ninety degrees so that you end up in the south, facing South.

Step 4 :

Now in the South, repeat Step 1 and Step 2, but vibrate:

"Adonai", pronounced *Ah-Doh-Nye*

Step 5 :

Draw the brilliant white line connecting the pentagram in the south to the west. Repeat Step 1 and Step 2, but vibrate:

"EHEIEH", pronounced *Eh-Heh-Yeh*

Step 6 :

Draw the brilliant white line connecting the pentagram in the West to the North. Now in the North, repeat Step 1 and Step 2, but vibrate:

"Agla", pronounced *Ah-Glah*

Complete the circle by connecting a white line from the north to the east where you began. Then, moving in the same clockwise direction, return to where you started the ritual. You should once again be facing east. If you do not have room for a circle, simply pivot where you stand.

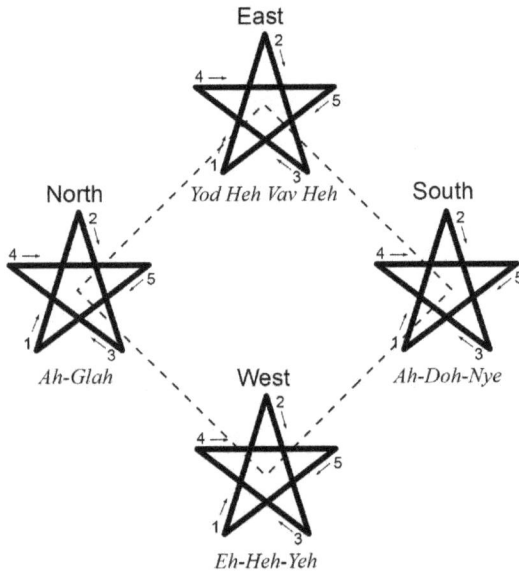

Illustration 4: Lesser Banishing Ritual of the Pentagram

225

Step 7 :

Now visualize the brilliant white circle expanding up and down to form a sphere above, below and all around you. What you have done is created a sphere in brilliant white all around you with electric blue pentagrams at the quarters which have been charged and sealed with God names.

Exercise: The Evocation of the Archangels

Step 1:

Stretch your arms straight out to the sides, so that your body forms a cross. Take a second or two to once again feel the energies that you felt when performing the Kabbalistic Cross. Re-create a cross of light within your being (the cross also represents the four archetypal elements: Air, Earth, Fire and Water).

Step 2:

Say: "Before me, (vibrate) Rah-fay-el."

Visualize the Archangel Raphael on a hill in front of you. He is dressed in a yellow robe which has purple highlights. He carries a Caduceus Wand (the symbol used by doctors, a wand entwined by serpents, which represents the life force). Feel a breeze coming from behind him.

Step 3:

Say: "Behind me, (vibrate) Gah-bree-el."

Visualize Archangel Gabriel behind you, dressed in blue with some orange highlights. The figure holds a cup and is surrounded by waterfalls or the ocean. Try to feel the moisture in the air.

Step 4:

Say: "On my right, (vibrate) Mee-chai-el."

Visualize the Archangel Michael dressed in a scarlet red robe with green highlights. He is holding a flaming sword. Feel the qualities of fire emanating from him.

Step 5:

Say: "And on my left, (vibrate) Oh-ree-el."

Visualize the Archangel Auriel dressed in Earth tones on a fertile landscape. He holds a bundle of wheat.

Step 6:

After you have invoked the Archangels move your feet slightly apart, still with both arms stretched out to the sides. Now visualize yourself within a large pentagram and say:

"For before me flames the pentagram."

"And behind me shines the six-rayed star."

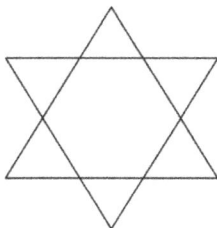

*Illustration 5: Six-rayed
Star*

Step 7:

Repeat the Kabbalistic Cross

Other people have different versions of the Evocation to the Archangels. In one version you would say, "Around me flames the pentagram, behind me shines the six-rayed star". There are little differences between what is said, but you might like to try them and see which works best for you.

Archangel Names and Their Meanings:

In the East: Raphael, God has healed.

In the West: Gabriel, God is my strength.

In the South: Michael, Who is as God.

In the North: Auriel, Light of God.

Note: There are many people who perform this ritual that have problems visualizing. If you are one who has problems seeing visual pictures, just know in your mind that it is there. For example, as with the pentagrams, although you may not be able to see the lines or the color being in brilliant blue, just affirm to yourself that it is there.

Some will encounter that they have problems feeling the energies. Don't worry, this is common. One reason that this may be occurring is that you may not be accustomed to the ritual so the energies it invokes may be too foreign to you. It just takes time and persistence to work through this. On a more positive note, those who think of themselves as being "numb" will be glad to know that over a long period of performing the L.B.R.P. daily, your sphere of sensation is slowly but surely becoming accustomed to the energies. So when you have internally reached a state of openness, you then you will feel the presence of the Archangels as truly powerful and present.

ADDITIONAL RESOURCES FROM LAW OF ATTRACTION SOLUTIONS, LLC.

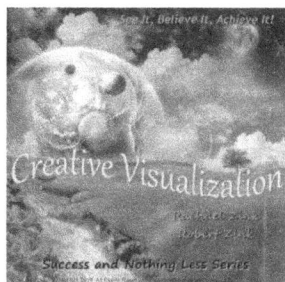

Creative Visualization is a meditative guide to manifesting the life you desire. Do you desire success and nothing less? Creative Visualization can help you achieve this. As you use creative visualization for just 20 to 30 minutes a day, you will see continued manifestation in your daily life. Get the life you have always dreamed of, learn the Four Fold Breath, stay calm with the Relaxation Ritual, and begin the empowering process of Creative Visualization.

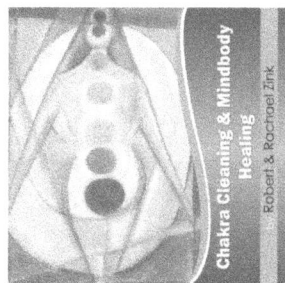

Blossom like a lotus flower with the **Chakra Cleaning & Mindbody Healing Program.** This easy to use program quickly helps you clean, clear, and refresh your chakras. You will be amazed at the opportunities you will attract with clean chakras. This program will raise your vibration so you attract the life you dream of. It will also aid you in healing your relationships and building a foundation of unconditional love in your life.

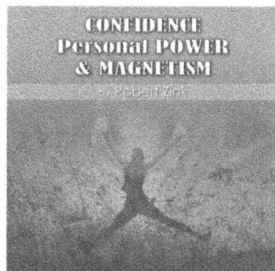

Confidence, Personal Power & Magnetism is a hypnotic guide to manifesting confidence. Do you desire success and nothing less? Begin raising your confidence, learn 24 confidence techniques, and be empowered by the Hypnotic Confidence Accelerator. As you use the skills for Building Confidence and the daily Claiming Confidence Exercise, you will see your personal power grow.

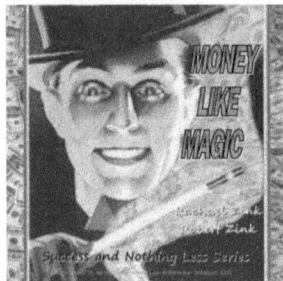

Start attracting **Money Like Magic.** It's a fact that most people want more money. All the latest evidence on wealth building shows that the only difference between the wealthy and the poor is *BELIEFS*. This easy to use program quickly helps you attract money and build wealth by transforming both your *conscious* and *subconscious* money beliefs. Are you ready for Money Like Magic?!?

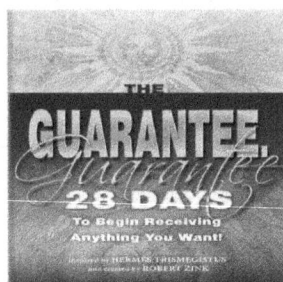

Imagine, you could begin attracting anything you want within 28 days. **The Guarantee** reveals ancient secrets based on the teachings of the Emerald Tablet of Hermes. The Guarantee will help you transform your life using the proven alchemical stages of life mastery as taught by the ancient mystery schools. Learn how to master the Law of Attraction through powerful, easy to do exercises.

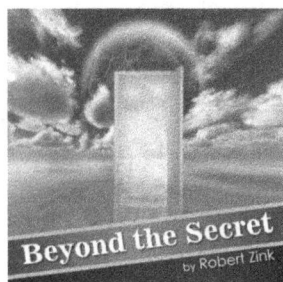

The Law of Attraction is every bit as real as the law of gravity. The law of gravity is a necessity for survival of the human race, but can also prove painful. The same is true with the Law of Attraction. **Beyond the Secret** shows you how to get beyond the limitations of the "The Secret" allowing your intentions to begin flowing into your life now.

All of these incredible instantly downloadable MP3s programs and MORE are available at www.lawofattractionsolutions.com.

www.ingramcontent.com/pod-product-compliance
Lightning Source LLC
Chambersburg PA
CBHW022015090426
42739CB00006BA/137